LONG AND SHORT OF IT

[handwritten inscription]

At the request of the author, all proceeds from the
sale of this book are to be donated to BLESMA
(British Limbless Ex-Service Men's Association).

LONG AND SHORT OF IT

ERIC COTTAM

COUNTRY BOOKS

Published by:
Country Books
Courtyard Cottage, Little Longstone, Bakewell, Derbyshire DE45 1NN

ISBN 1 898941 65 3

Printed and bound by MFP Design & Print

DEDICATION

If anyone finds this, I love you.

PROLOGUE

With a caution learned in recent weeks, I opened my eyes without moving – and then had the peculiar feeling of waking up and not knowing where I was. A strange room slowly took shape. A high, white ceiling was the first thing I saw, and it seemed promising. Furthermore, I was lying in a bed that had clean white sheets and pillow slips. Screens surrounded the bed and squared off a corner of what seemed a hospital ward. It had the clean, antiseptic smell of one. The dimmed artificial lighting indicated that it was night-time, and the stillness suggested the small hours, but I didn't know what day it was, or even the month.

A head was poking through a small opening in the screens at the foot of the bed. It was perched on a neck that had a white band of collar above a starkly contrasting black background. The significance of the intruder's clerical garb did not strike me at the time.

The seemingly unsupported head had slicked-back dark hair that shone dully in the pale light reflected from the white ceiling. The face was creamy smooth, calm, expressionless. Eyes peering out of the head glanced over me – up and down. Why down, only my head was visible?

The thin, delicate nose wrinkled in distaste at the confined stench of gangrenous wounds. Days must have passed since I had had even a quick wash so I reeked also of grime, stale sweat and urine. I sourly resented being reminded that I stank.

Bravely, the mouth opened. "What is your name?" The lips

quivered in expectancy of an instant reply.

"Cottam, Private Cottam, 2nd Battalion Royal Warwickshire ..."

"And your address?" the mouth interrupted with a faintly offensive nuance of authority. "Your home address?"

I told him, dismissing the request as normal procedure. The loud silence that followed made me feel embarrassed about speaking with him, but questions were beginning to line up in my mind.

Bracing myself, I asked abruptly: "Where am I?"

"Netley Hospital, Southampton," the voice countered.

A wave of relief swept over me. Comforted, I was about to ask him: "How did I get here?" But he gave me no more of his precious time.

"Well – cheerio – and good luck," the mouth said haltingly before my own had a chance to open again. As if it had been held there on the end of a pole, the head withdrew. It had seen, it had smelt, it had asked, it had heard, it had wished me good luck knowing that good luck was going to be needed for something, and now it had gone.

I slept and dreamt that I could not get my breath. I was suffocating and life was being crushed out of me. I awoke feeling inexplicably different in the bed with its clean white sheets and pillow-slips. I was now wearing a pyjama jacket – my first ever. I must have been attended to while asleep. The screens had been removed.

Ointment soothed the left side of my face, and my left elbow had been bandaged and had stiffened. My right wrist had been dressed and was feeling sore: the frayed, teased ends of catgut, which had been hurriedly severed at a forward field casualty clearing station, had turned it septic.

Spanning my midriff and extending to almost the end of the bed was an inserted wire cage that domed the bedclothes, preventing them from lying directly on my wounded legs. A linen screen, tied to the front rim of this cradle and to the tubular sides of the bed, prevented me from looking down the formed tunnel when lifting the bedclothes. I thought dully that it was something to do with the surgical dressings.

Though I had not seen anyone except the head on a pole, I was no longer distressed, hungry and thirsty, as had been my lot recently. Now freed of pain, I felt grateful for still being alive with my short, inglorious war apparently over. The Belgium Campaigne, which had degenerated into chaotic shambles, into an unending nightmare, must also be over – with an adverse conclusion.

I felt sad when I thought about 'H', our likeable sergeant. And what had happened to the others in the platoon? Long afterwards, it was admitted officially that of the total strength of the Battalion, over 800 men, only a disproportionate 137 of them had waded out to the pitching boats to be taken to the waiting destroyers lying off Dunkirk.

Dawn was beckoning. The sentinel, low-powered ceiling lights allowed me to see that my bed was in a corner of a big and airy ward, and that it was irregularly spaced farther apart from the next one in the row. There was an opposite row of mounded beds. I slept and did not dream.

I awoke later in the morning to find the ward bustling with activity. The busily engaged nurses wore the instantly recognisable grey uniform dresses of the elite Queen Axexandra's Royal Army Nursing Corps (Quarancs) under their white bib aprons. One of them, a very composed young sister, asked me how I felt.

"All right, thank you, sister," I mumbled self-consciously. She took my pulse and temperature, entered the details on the clipboard hanging on the end rail of the bcd and then gave me a searching look.

"An orderly will wash and shave you and give you a bottle. When did you last have your bowels open?"

"I can't remember," I answered truthfully, embarrassed by the basic question.

Again, she gave me a strange look, as if she was trying to read my thoughts. "We'll see what happens in the next day or two. If nothing does, we shall have to give you an enema."

The sister had spoken kindly but her whole attitude was

markedly professional. She had drawn a demarcation line that I, a private soldier, would not be permitted to cross.

The male orderly had left me looking and feeling presentable when a robust Army chaplain strode purposefully into the ward and veered to my bedside. The chaplain told me my mother had been informed by his civilian colleague of my arrival at Netley Hospital. However, because of war-time restrictions governing travel by train, her visit would be delayed. In the meantime he would arrange temporary accommodation for her, he said. I thought it was unusually kind of a stranger to do this for me.

The next morning, after breakfast, the young sister told me that my dressings would have to be changed. Sister and nurse rolled up the bed clothes from the foot of the bed and sat them on the top of the cage. From each side of the bed gloved hands disappeared between exposed ribs of the cage, returning to the mid-positioned surgical trolley. Their movements were wary, furtive, causing me no discomfort but making me feel a little uneasy, particularly as the nurses seemed disinclined to chat with their new patient.

Rolling back the bed clothes, the nurses redraped the cage. Their task completed, the trolley was wheeled towards another bedside and the tiny rattles of little bottles and the silvery tinkles of surgical instruments lying in enamel dishes framed an imposed silence. Before disturbing their next patient the sister shot me a half glance over her shoulder and then whispered something to the nurse.

The tapes securing the linen screen to the sides of my bed had become loosened. I felt it my duty to re-tie them. I struggled to a sitting position, careful to avoid moving my heavily numbed legs. Feeling a little dizzy I steadied myself by laying the palms of my hands on the curved, unyielding raised bed clothes. I lifted up the bed clothes and folded them over the top of the cage. Before re-tying the screen I would gratify a mild curiosity and look behind it at my legs.

I lifted the screen, and stared with a growing, then lingering disbelief at the white sheet glaring back at me.

CHAPTER 1

"Tarrah, *mate* – see you!" cried Len as he jumped onto the platform of a slow-moving-bus.

"You shall, when *I'm* eighteen!" I shouted up at him.

He swivelled on the bright metal pole and half waved with his free hand. His finely chiselled face barely maintained a set expression. Unusually, he seemed a little apprehensive. His bus merged with the flowing traffic. Feeling a big pit forming inside me, I turned for home.

I would miss the lively company of my pugnacious, Jimmy Cagney-like mate at evenings and weekends. He had become my closest friend since we had first met, or rather clashed, in the stores of a factory where we both had worked as labourers. He had been patiently waiting his turn to weigh his loaded workpan of finished machine parts when I had beaten him to it by quickly sliding my workpan onto the unsteadied platform of the weighing machine.

Barely controlling his temper, Len yelled at me, "Hang on, *mate*, I was here before you!"

He habitually used the comradely term, and would emphasise it when feeling not particularly matey. I didn't know that then, and I was also unaware that he was an amateur boxer. His skewed nose should have warned me not to tangle with him. Fortunately, Len had not insisted on his rightful priority.

Despite Len's short temper, we never really fell out during the two years we had known each other, although we were opposites in some ways. We complemented each other. We were a double act.

Len had worked only in the one factory since leaving school at the age of fourteen, whereas I had drifted from one factory job to another since leaving school at the same age. Len had known only one house, the one in which he was born. I had known many but cannot remember the one in which I was born being too young when the family moved from it. I didn't catch up with our houses until we came to live in an isolated one near Abergavenny.

Len had been biding his time. Unlike me, he had a subconscious aim in life, which had surfaced. It was startling news he confided to me that late Sunday afternoon as we cycled home, two abreast, from Evesham.

"I'm going to enlist, he said. "Don't tell anyone just yet. Ma should be the first to know."

I should have realised that he was destined for the Army. Since the Depression, every male member of his Victorian-sized family had 'gone for a soldier', just as soon as they were old enough. Those of his many, elder brothers who were not at present serving in the Army, had been honourably discharged (time served) from it. Now, the Army was claiming the last of that generation of the family.

I hadn't reflected seriously on my aimless life until Len had decided to enlist. I was still adding to the list of factories where once I had worked, some big, some small, changing jobs as soon as boredom set in. On the way to the bus stop with Len I had planned my future, at least, the first seven years of it. I also would join up.

Before returning home, I called at Len's, a terraced two-up-and-two-down in a dismal back street of Balsall Heath, a fug-canopied suburb of Birmingham. The long row of old, sorry, uniform houses, robbed of filtered sunlight by tall factories on the other side of the narrow street, was tunnelled at regular intervals by arched entries that led to communal back yards. Front door steps, concaved by the tread of countless feet over many years, protruded and squatted solidly on the pavement and made you raise a knee every few steps as you walked down the street.

With the customary warning knock on the door I stepped

straight into the living room. As expected, Len's mother was in. She rarely went out, not even to shop. That task had been delegated to her two youngest daughters, who were now the last of her many children who still lived at home. The girls were factory workers, as were most workers in the city of a thousand and one trades, where everything was made, from motor cars to cosmetic jewellery, from bicycles to 'cheap tin trays'.

"Not wairkin', Eric?" Ma raised her cloudy eyes from the flickering coal fire she was stirring with a knobby poker.

"Not this afternoon – I saw Len off."

Still clutching the poker in a gnarled, arthritic hand she thanked me with a slow smile. I sat down on the opposite easy chair. The only other items of furniture in the shaded living room were a horse-hair stuffed sofa, two stools and a badly scratched walnut-veneered china cabinet.

Ma had brought up her large, finely spaced family in this small house. Her many sons had slept sardine fashion while waiting to be creamed off by the Army. The prematurely aged lady now enjoyed a matriarchal role in this once cramped household. Her own daily tasks soon completed she would sit quietly in her wide armchair staring fixedly at the ever-changing picture of a flaming fire, the leaping yellows and spurting blues streaking through upwardly spiralling grey smoke.

Sensing my mood, Ma said, "I'll make a pot of tea."

Hearing her clattering crockery to attention in the tiny kitchen I put a few odd copper coins in the japan-lacquered tea caddy that sat on the mantelpiece between two of Len's amateur boxing trophies – little silver cups. The caddy held the weekly contributions from visiting married sons and daughters and from those living at home. The accumulated contents of the little tin box would pay for Ma's annual day trip to Blackpool, her one big treat of the year. Amazingly, many of her female contemporaries in the district had never even seen the sea. They had to be content with a reluctant promise of a rare outing on an open-topped tram, to Lickey Hills: "If it doesn't rain."

Ma staggered along the pattern-erased path in the lino bearing

13

the teapot and two mugs, in which milk and sugar had been added unequally, on a chipped enamelled tray that flamboyantly advertised a local beer.

"Dad out?" I declared as much as asked, knowing that he would be.

"He's always out," she confirmed quietly without bitterness.

When I first visited Len's, his father, a wiry little man, who had refused to wear his new false teeth, had just retired from work. He afterwards had shrunk anonymously into the background. Even when he was in, he wasn't: he would be outside the back door tinkering at his ancient bike or fiddling with his fishing tackle. Every day, except when the weather was foul, he was out on his bike with his fishing rod tied to the cross bar.

When he was younger he also had used his fists: to teach his young boys the noble art; to control his lads when they resented control; to defend himself against any of his grown-up sons whenever he had reeled home drunk and upset their mother. That was a younger, fiery Dad. Old Dad was an amiable little bloke who would sit placidly on a river bank fishing, with his empty mouth open.

"You'll miss Len?" Ma enquired and waited for me to admit it.

"I shall. We've knocked about for a couple of years. Feel strange at week-ends without him. But I'll join him in two month's time."

"All your lads were in the Army, Ma." Again, it was a statement rather than a question. I wanted confirmation that it was not unusual for young men to enlist.

"Two of them are still in. Joe's in India and Ben's in Aldershot," she said. "All the young men round 'ere join the Army. Waym loik the Gairkhas," Ma said in her pure Brummie accent. She had spent all her life in the city, most of it in this street.

By contrast, my mother had roamed widely as her family increased. Her four sons were born on those travels; interspersed with the boys were four girls, but they all died in childbirth. The birth certificates of her eight children are miles apart from each other.

Just after being widowed, my mother moved her family from Stourbridge, in Worcestershire, to Birmingham. Tony, the eldest son, who was two years older than myself, and I had previously travelled by train to work there in a factory, one that made rectangular coal scuttles. The move to the city saved the cost of our rail fares. In adapting to our new environment we *became* 'Brummies'.

"I'd better go. I'll pop round now and then?" I suggested to Ma.

"I'll be glad to see you. I think Ruth would be, too," Ma hinted with a knowing smile. I felt myself redden. Ruth was the 'baby' of the family. She was sixteen and a little taller than Len and much nearer to my height. She was an attractive girl with a slender figure and rich auburn hair. I had been thinking about her.

"I'll take a look at the bike before going home," I said off-handedly to cover my embarrassment at being caught out.

I left through the back door that led onto the blue-brick paved courtyard. The courtyard was separated from an identical one on either side by a row of communal lavatories and wash houses. Graded toilet papers torn from the *Daily Mirror* and the *Birmingham Mail* hung in the lavatories. Portable tin baths hung in the adjacent wash-houses. Propped against the brick encased copper boiler in the wash-house that Ma shared with a next-door neighbour, was our old Triumph motor bike.

Len and I had rescued the bike from a scrapheap and had patiently restored it to a stuttering working order. We couldn't ride it on the road – it wasn't licensed, neither were we – so we rode it, in turns, 'wall of death' fashion round the sentinel lamppost in the centre of the bowl-like, sunken courtyard becoming practically invisible in self-generated smoke screens. Ma's near neighbours, and those who lived in the opposite line of terraced houses whose back doors also faced the yard, were amused at first by our restricted antics. The eruption of staccato roars of the engine on quiet Sunday afternoons as we circled the lamppost chased by blue smoke belching from the exhaust, caused their tolerant smiles to turn to scowls, and then to unlovely snarls of disapproval.

"If," as one of them put it sarcastically, "we want to watch speedway, we'll go to Perry Barr."

Still thinking about Len, I kick-started the bike with the intention of doing a couple of laps round the lamppost maypole. As the engine spluttered to an echoing wakefulness a disembodied male voice bellowed from out of an unfriendly doorway: "Don't you dare ride that bloody thing round this yard otherwise I'll throw it out into the street and you with it!"

I didn't recognise the voice, but he sounded bigger than me so I killed the engine and then slunk home.

Our own poorly furnished old house was just round the corner. The front room had been converted into a fish and chip shop by the previous hopeful tenant and my mother had taken over the business. It had been Mam's third attempt to revive a failed fish and chip shop since we arrived in the city. Like the previous two, it had been opened with a breezy optimism for, Mam stoutly maintained, there was a 50% profit to be made on fish and chips. This might be true when a reasonable amount of them is sold, but it never was. The family was our shop's best customer. Like the previous two, the business flopped and the neglected fish ranges quietly stagnated behind a front door that was permanently closed to the general public, and once again we returned to eating main meals that now only occasionally needed flavouring with malt vinegar. Eventually the clothes we wore stopped reeking of stale cotton seed oil, but the smell of it sulked obstinately in the front room where Mam's three eldest sons now garaged their bikes.

Between attempts to rejuvenate tired fish and chip shops, Mam had cheaply rented large, decaying old houses to accommodate lodgers. We were relentlessly moving to and from shops and from and to lodging houses, usually just ahead of insistent rent collectors. Sometimes, to quell the mounting concern of gossipy neighbours, an unrelated lodger would become an 'uncle'.

I often wondered why Mam never married again. She was then in her early forties. She was not beautiful but she was undeniably attractive, and intelligent. Her slate-grey eyes were deeply set in her roundish face and she had a trim figure. She could not settle, though. Now freed from the few restraints of her marriage she had become even more shiftless.

Mam was born in the Black Country, as it was then aptly called. She won a scholarship to Halesowen Grammar School. At eighteen, equipped with a Higher School Certificate that embraced music and French, she became a teacher at a village school in Shropshire. My father (elect) was a local farm labourer. The saturnine Edward and the spirited Nell met, married and were doomed to live in virtual poverty ever afterwards.

Since his late teens Dad suffered with pulmonary tuberculosis. He died of this unrelenting disease after reaching his fortieth birthday, just before I had my fourteenth. He had never been a healthy man since I first became aware of him. For the last seven years of his life he was confined permanently to his bed. Daily, a hole in his right side had to be unplugged and fluid drained off. Mam was almost always compelled to take over the task from busy district nurses. Dad's bedrooms were littered with bandages, gauze, white enamel kidney bowls with blue rims and dark green fluted bottles of Eusol, a new antiseptic with a unique smell.

Dad had been, in succession, a farm labourer, unemployed, an insurance agent, something mysterious, a bailiff, a bread roundsman and, finally, a door-to-door salesman. That was the last time I saw my strong-willed father upright, his tall, thin frame sagging under the weight of a very heavy sample case that was crammed full of brushes. He then became bedridden and wasted away physically to a caricature of his former self. He became a presence, one who had little contact with his sons.

In those bleak years, whenever Mam fell ill, her husband was returned to hospital and her four children were clapped in orphanages until she recovered. That brief account of our early family life may explain why we were never a close, openly affectionate family. It seemed as if we had been thrown together and that we all were trying to make the best of it. We were a family of individuals having a strange mutual dependency. Though we loved one another, we did not always like each other.

I was dwelling on the past and what the future held for us all, thoughts triggered by Len's departure, when Mam bustled in from work. She was surprised to see me at home, sitting glumly, elbows on the table, holding my cheeks between my palms.

"You're home early. You haven't hurt yourself again?" She surveyed me dispassionately, looking for clues such as a blood-stained bandage. I assured her that I hadn't.

My poor factory safety record had prompted the anxious question. I hadn't been back at work very long having had two months off with a broken big toe caused by resolving a violent disagreement with a fellow hot-press stamper. We had used our big ram-adjusting spanners as two-handed clubs and had tried to maim each other. On surrendering, my opponent, with a feigned contempt, had flung down his 'weapon'. It landed on my foot. I had both won and lost.

Previously, at another factory, while operating a crude milling machine, I had nearly lost my left hand when it was whirled around the dangerously exposed singing circular saw for a split second. My badly lacerated hand laid me off work for six months.

Mam, scenting easy money, had sought compensation for this injury. With me in tow she visited a Poor Mans' Lawyer. Our legal adviser, a pallid, thin-lipped member of his profession, was nobly enduring a voluntary stint after normal office hours. He was sitting behind a huge polished desk and his hands were placed together, fingers to lips, in an attitude of prayer as we entered his office. He wrenched his gaze from a wall clock and nodded vaguely at two vacated chairs.

Prominently displayed on the desk, comfortably within reach of those seeking free legal advice from the PML Organisation, was a large DONATION BOX, so it read. Anticipating four lemons, Mam inserted a coin into the presumptuous box.

Mam explained to the emotionally cold lawyer the reason for our visit and thrust forward Exhibit A, my maimed mitt. It did at least extract from him, on the recoil, a wince of repugnance.

"I should like to press a claim for compensation," Mam added formally in a resurrected middle-class tone of voice.

With a frown, and a pretended smile the lawyer explained that claims for compensation for my kind of injury were very difficult to pursue. He said it was simpler if something was obviously missing when claiming compensation for an industrial accident. Amputated fingers, for instance, would be assessed on a sliding scale, so much for each joint or joints lost – always providing, of course, that personal negligence was not proven.

Unco-operatively, I had retained my entire, now mutilated, hand including the little finger that had been almost severed and has ever since remained partially numbed. Mam's expected four lemons, when they turned up, were not all in the same row.

When I was off work through injuries my sole income was meagre panel money, just ten shillings a week, which barely kept me. Like most families in the district, we were not well off so it was necessary for me to earn a reasonable wage. Mam was simply being pragmatic when she enquired about my welfare.

"I took the afternoon off to be with Len," I announced. "He's joined up. He should be in Warwick now." I let the news sink in.

"I thought he would one day – it runs in the family. Must admit I liked having him around the place – he's such a cheerful lad."

Len revered all mothers and he got on particularly well with mine. Mam was fond of him. She was probably fond of her own sons, but she never expressed her fondness for the three youngest of them. There was a rare display of muted affection for Tony and now Len, who had become one of the family, as I had become part of his.

Mam brushed aside some dirty crockery, relics of the last, hasty meal scattered on the oil-cloth covered kitchen table that was everlastingly laid for meals. She stood her bulging shopping bag on the cleared space and started to empty it, then paused and looked from the opened bag to me as though struck by a sudden thought. "You're not thinking about the Army, are you?"

"I'm not old enough," I said, dodging the anticipated question.

"You soon will be," she said accusingly with a piercing look.

"We'll see when –"

"Are you?" she persisted. Her hand gripped an extracted 2lb. bag of sugar. The contents of the stiff blue paper bag grated under an extra pressure.

19

"Yes, I am," I said, half-directing my answer to the floor.

She looked at me as if she was seeing me in a new light. "Can't you wait until next year when Dai leaves school and gets a job? His wages would almost replace yours."

David was the youngest of my three brothers. He was born in Cardiff, where we once lived, and he answered to the Welsh version of his name. Next year he would leave elementary school, whichever one he was then attending. He had known many, as did his three elder brothers in the nomadic family. It was astounding we learnt anything. Next year, Dai would be wearing dungarees.

"I'd like to do something other than working in factories," I said, again avoiding the direct question. "The Army might teach me a trade."

Mam pulled out a Woodbine, lit it, and sat down. After doing Dad's daily dressing she had taken to smoking a cigarette. She retained the habit and passed it on to each of her sons in turn. That was our excuse.

"You could become a tradesman in a factory, a toolsetter, a toolmaker," she said, the fag waggling as she spoke. It would smoulder in her mouth until reduced to a small butt, then taken out for the first and last time. Sometimes the burning butt would be used to light another.

"It may be possible even though I'm old for an apprenticeship, but I would earn a poor wage until at least twenty one." That was the only time Mam suggested that I did something better than semi-skilled factory work.

"Suit yourself," she said dismissively with a resigned shrug of her shoulders. Talking to a wall had evidently come to her mind. Rising from the chair she resumed emptying her bag. Then, in a dismayed tone of voice she said: "I'd have thought you'd wait until Dai brings in a wage. We are just getting straight with you back at work." Defiantly, an inch-length of ash clung tenaciously to its waggling base.

Dai would be at school for the next sixteen months. I was not willing to wait so long, though she had now made me feel that I would be deserting her. She had held on to her children through difficult times, extricating them from orphanages and caring for them in scrambled-together new homes. But sixteen months! During that time how many more factories would turn me into a robotic machine operator? My mind was made up. I would enlist in two month's time, on my eighteenth birthday.

Despite her scholastic background, Mam had never encouraged any of her sons educationally. When we left elementary school she had never suggested evening classes to us so that we could qualify for something better than factory work. Now aware that Mam's care of us bordered on unintentional neglect, I did not feel so guilty about my intention to leave home for a new life.

"We're having kippers tonight," Mam said. Her voice then came back to trumpet strength. "Get out the frying pan!" she bawled to Dai who had just come in from school. He widened his stuck faint smile on seeing me at home earlier than usual and yanked out the blackened pan from underneath the stacked saucepans in a cupboard.

Dai and I were bigger built than the eldest son, Tony, and the next youngest son, Bill. Those two brothers were small and compact and were not to match us physically. Mam's four boys were paired. The even numbers, my pair, were comparatively easy going. The other pair, the brains of the brood, were intensely serious lads.

Mam, when she was not frying fish and chips or putting up boarders, worked in a factory. Her sons, except Dai of course, were also factory workers. Tony engraved steel rules; I was then beading the bulbous front wings of Humber Super Snipes, which later became the staff cars of the British Army; Bill was grinding the bevels on large mirrors; Mam was spot-welding automobile components. Of all her many factory jobs, capstan operator, solderer, pressworker, etc., spot-welding was the one she best liked doing.

An enchanting sepia-tinted photograph has been unearthed showing Mam with her dignified colleagues at their Shropshire village school just before the Great War. They had submitted themselves to the photographer uneasily as they sat in the playground in professionally graded lines flowing symmetrically from each side of the stern-looking headmaster. They posed formally as if for a portrait painting. Mam was wearing a puffed-up blouse and a straw hat in the boater style and had assumed the dignified manner befitting the occasion. She might have sat nearer to the headmaster on future photographs. Instead, she became a spot-welder, which raised a few eyebrows in those class-conscious days.

Bill strolled in from work, just ahead of Tony. 'Sweet William', as we referred to him when he was anything but, sniffed the air and said: "One-eyed steaks again," as the pan hissed and dispensed an aroma that would pervade the whole house and fight for supremacy of the front room.

"It's all we can afford. And it will be bacon and eggs tomorrow when we'll do without the yoiking and squawking, you sarcastic little sod." Mam rarely brought home the language of work, but Bill's acid tongue often reminded her of a need to. With a contemptuous curl of his upper lip he pulled up a chair and sat down.

Tony, my quiet, studious eldest brother, inspected his kipper and then reached for a slice of buttered bread. Catching my eye he said, "You off on your bike this Sunday, Owkid?"

"No. Len's joined up. I'll go to the park. Might get a game of football."

"Army, as did his brothers, or Navy?"

"Army – Royal Warwickshire Regiment."

"I would have preferred the Air Force."

"So would I," chipped in Bill "I would like to learn to fly one of the new fighter planes."

"You may get the chance if Hitler carries on much longer," Mam prophesied. "Don't give fish bones to Judy," this was said to Dai who was dangling the long, feathery spine of his kipper temptingly above the investigating nose of our mongrel dog. "They will stick in her throat." Judy looked upward appealingly at Dai, then at Mam and then longingly at the filleted bone as it was returned to the plate.

Our affectionate, intelligent mongrel dog was fox-like, two-tone brown with a little tail curled resolutely forward over her back. Quick, responsive, she was sensitive to changes of mood of any of her family. Judy had been Dad's dog, given to him as a pup to provide a little lively company in his isolated sick room. Judy retreated to her rug underneath the organ from where she could see and not be noticed.

Hard against the wall, this old pedal organ loomed over the kitchen table where we were seated. It had been found reclining, in pieces, in the coal cellar where it had been consigned by the previous tenant. Helped by Len, Tony and I had carried the disassembled organ back up the cellar steps. Brummies being to the spanner born we had reassembled the old wind-operated instrument, fitting the blanched pieces of fretted and ornate woodwork, the air bellows and the graded in length pipes.

Restored to its rightful position in the kitchen-cum-living room, where once it had overpowered religious meetings, its curvy outline mated up exactly with the blurred border that separated faded wallpaper from the greater area of exposed and grimy wallpaper. Our old sideboard had stood there for a short time and, being comparatively smaller in outline, had hinted that something larger had stood there previously. When the sideboard went, the organ rose up.

We could not persuade Mam to play it, so we settled for Len's entire musical repertoire, the piano exercise: da dee dum dum dum, da dee dum dum dum... The black-ringed, yellowed ivory pull-out stops could produce an amazing variety of softly flowing 'da dee dum dum dums'. After a performance, Judy would slink back to her bed.

The organ owed its recall to that oak sideboard, which had to be sold when we were very hard up. The well-travelled piece of furniture was our last tangible link with Dad, apart from Judy, and was probably the only piece our parents had not bought second-hand. During its many travels the framed vertical mirror on the top had suffered a crack. (I thought it better to admit this before someone spots it.)

Len and I had humped the very heavy sideboard to the second-hand furniture shop, the only one within humping distance. We hoped to agree a price for it that would save us having to hump it back. We were in Laurel and Hardy territory as we staggered along the busy street of tightly packed shops with our burden, our feet shuffling under the end rails. We had arranged beforehand that Len should conduct the sale with the dealer. Native to the district, Len knew most of the shopkeepers, including this one with whom he was on sneering terms.

"How much will you give us for this, mate?" Len asked breathlessly, bracing himself for trouble.

The stony-faced dealer was standing outside his shop and we had dropped our heavy load at his splayed feet. Returning the wet-ended fag to his mouth he rested his hand on the sideboard to see if it was supported freely on wobbly legs. Slowly removing the fag with a clutch of fingers, he deliberated and his face began to screw itself into the look he used for strangling the optimism in those who needed to sell him something.

"Thirty-five bob", he declared flatly.

Len was shocked. We had planned him to be, but now he wasn't acting. This was real. "It's worth at least fifty-five bob!" he gasped.

"With a cracked mirror?"

"Split the difference – forty-five?" said Len with a despairing look at me.

"Thirty seven-and-six."

"Forty two-and-six," said Len, and I felt that he was about to detonate.

"I'll give you two quid for it and no more," the dealer said hoarsely, and in went the fag. Len agonised for a moment and then capitulated. The dealer took a tight roll of banknotes from out of the top pocket of his soiled overall coat and peeled off two green ones. Reluctantly Len took the money.

"Help me to take it inside," the dealer said casually, naturally expecting assistance as he moved to one end of the sideboard.

"For two quid? Get stuffed, *mate!*"

CHAPTER 2

Mam maintained that anyone could find a job in Brum. That was why she had moved the family there.

Proving, yet again, that Mam was right, I exchanged pressed steel work for a job in an automobile component factory. Here my industrial path crossed with that of Mam's. After one unsettling and inhibiting week working near my mother, seeing her glow with pride at the sight of a heap of hot, coupled components that she had just mated with a spot welder, I left and began working in an armament factory.

During my short stay at this factory I was concerned with the invention of either Mr Lewis or that of Mr Vickers for I later learnt that the anonymous breech blocks I had slavishly fed in stages to a demanding bank of semi-auto milling machines were definitely not parts of Bren guns, the gas-operated light machine guns. The Bren gun, spawned in Czechoslovakia, had yet to be adopted by the British Army. Gun and I would together reinforce the defences of this country. Learning to strip a Bren gun down and then reassemble it, sometimes blindfolded to emulate darkness, made me familiar with its innards. It followed, therefore, that the breech blocks I had repetitiously machined, and which had left me soaked in suds oil, were the offsprings of either Lew or Vick.

I switched jobs for the last time.

As I crouched over the spinning chuck of a big capstan lathe, one of the girl press operators leant over my shoulder. "You're thinking of joining the Army, aren't you, Eric?" she cooed.

"Yes. Next week, on my birthday," I replied, straightening up and indexing the turret for the next operation.

"My Sid says it's a wonderful life. He's stationed in Alexandria. We're getting married when he comes home on leave". Her eyes were misting as she spoke. She showed me some photographs just received from Egypt. Her chap was variously posed, smartly dressed in his tropical whites when he wasn't wearing a bathing costume. Yes, it is a wonderful life, I agreed. One more week of machining brass castings and I'll be part of it, I thought.

I sincerely wished her the best of luck and hoped privately that if he was to continue hopping about those countries shown coloured red on a world atlas, she would be able to join him. She would then have an interesting life with him instead of spending her days monotonously feeding sheet brass into the maw of a blanking press.

She returned to her repetitive work singing a 'lurve' song. She would sing along with the other female press operators as they worked mechanically, the way of all factory piece-workers. Their harmonised singing would carry over the humming, whirring and clattering of the factory processes to fall gently on the tin ears of the males operating capstan lathes.

"Oiyam lownlee tewnoight...," she warbled as she returned to her press.

"So ammoy", I thought.

I called at the Army Recruiting Office in James Watt Street – a day late. A gang of workers with pneumatic drills was ploughing up the tarmac of the street. One of them had paused in his demolition work and was resting brown sinewy forearms with blue-grey tattooes on the handlebar of his idling drill. Spotting me as I slouched by he offered advice: "If you're about to join the Army," he bawled above the staccato hammering of his fellow drillers, "pull your shoulders back."

I ignored him. On entering the building, I straightened my lanky build to achieve my maximum height of five feet eight inches.

Anticipating a national emergency, there was an active recruiting campaign under way during that summer of 1938.

Blithely, I had assumed that the British Army would be delighted to welcome me into its extending ranks. Was I not young, fit, reasonably intelligent and, above all, expendable?

It was a false assumption. Kitchener's successors found that my country did not need me. I gathered that I had failed the medical examination, but nobody told me why I had failed. Nobody had a real wish to explain anything to me. They appeared to be too busy completing the forms of the three men who had passed the medical. I put my failure down to my injured left hand.

After enduring another month wrestling with a big capstan lathe at the brassfounders, I re-applied at the recruiting office. The desire to enlist had now become obsessive once the Army had refused to accept me. Though careful not to brandish my badly scarred hand, I was again turned down. This time the Army medical officer gave me a sealed note to take to my panel doctor. Presumably the note would explain the reason for my rejection. I did, just for a fleeting moment, consider steaming the letter open. But I dared not: it would have been a capital offence.

Dr. Cronin was a compassionate man. He said that all factory-working youths would lead a far healthier life in the Army and he would gladly help me to enlist. He sent me to Dudley Road Hospital to be examined by a specialist, as consultants were then called. I was given another sealed note and told to report to the out-patients' department.

A tired-looking sister referred to me indifferently as another one for 'Bones and Muscles.' Mr. Donovan was bones and muscles. This was to be our second meeting.

He had fixed my broken big toe caused by an opponent downing his improvised heavy weapon upon it after we had been duelling to settle an argument. Mr. Donovon, in describing an unusual fracture to a phalanx of medical students, had prodded my toe on turning his attention from the suspended shadowy x-rays to my blue-patched foot and I had found it difficult to dampen my involuntary muscular movements.

"Kindly endeavour to remain still," he snapped at me as he carried out his examination (prodding). My entire foot was afterwards cemented in plaster and I was given a present of a pair of wooden crutches to take home with me.

This day the spry specialist was in an affable mood and he didn't snap at me. He was eerily polite and addressed me as Mister. I had become his original discovery. He had a new entourage of medical students to whom to display the abnormal. I loaned them my body for examination. Pairs of intensely curious eyes targeted my bared chest.

It seemed that my father had bequeathed me a memento of his fatal illness. He had had his entire right lung removed in an attempt to stem the advance of pulmonary tuberculosis by leaping surgically in front of it. Consequently, he never regained the full use of his right arm and the associated pectoral muscles wasted. Nature responded to this neglect by making one of his son's right pectoral muscles non-functioning.

Mr. Donovan explained this in lofty medical terms to his respectful audience. I got the gist of his remarks. Apparently it was a rare hereditary condition. Because Mam made a joke about this flaw in my otherwise good physique, the medical term for it was soon erased from my memory.

Mr. Donovan found me an interesting case. I felt that his verdict was a personal reprimand. I began to see myself as a physically inferior specimen.

Turning to me, the specialist pronounced me otherwise fit and healthy. That uplifted my spirits a little. "However," he said, "in view of a possibly weakened right shoulder, you would perhaps be better suited to the Tank Corps. Enrolling in an infantry regiment would entail using a rifle, and that might prove too much of a strain on that shoulder."

I was grateful to him for telling me this. Specialists did not normally disclose their opinions directly to patients of panel doctors.

The great man was proved wrong about my shoulder. I became, eventually, a company shot on both rifle and Bren gun. Later, I was put down for a young soldiers' team to shoot at Bisley, but the outbreak of war froze such competitions. Sorry, I really am jumping the gun.

I did not want to join the Tank Corps, even if they offered to take me. Len had enlisted in an infantry unit and I wanted to join him. But how?

Len came home on his first leave. In just three months the Army had transformed him. He had lost his factory pallor and was tanned, rugged and had that undefinable but quite unmistakable air of healthiness denoting an active, mainly outdoor life. He had put on muscled weight. Adopting a mock fighting pose and snaking out a left he said modestly, "Featherweight now, can't make bantam let alone fly."

There was a psychological change in him, too. He was more in control of himself.

I envied him and was slightly embarrassed to be seen in his uniformed presence feeling that I contrasted unfavourably. I was taller than Len but now weighed less than him.

We strolled through Calthorpe Park. It was a brilliant summer day and there were very few people about. Though it was very hot Len would not undo the top brass button of his tunic. He carried a Malacca-cane. It is to keep hands out of pockets, he said. Swathed in khaki, peaked hat, uniform, puttees, and shod in highly polished black boots that complemented a startling white belt, Len was conspicuouosly and inhibitingly a soldier on leave.

We were muttering to each other about something or other as we walked slowly along a path when Len raised my hopes about enlisting. He halted, turned and rested the silver knob of his cane on my shoulder. He had been in deep thought and had suddenly hit upon a bright idea. He smiled vibrantly at me and tapped his message.

"Why not," he suggested, "why not apply to enlist at the Depot? Even if they find something wrong with you, they might be prepared to overlook it."

The regiment's depot was Budbrooke Barracks, near Warwick. I cycled to the barracks, found the separated recruiting office and was greeted by a recruiting sergeant who wore a splendid, colourful dress uniform. His smart turnout seemed to suggest that here the standards of entry into the regiment were even higher than those at James Watt Street.

The old doctor who medically examined me appeared to be spending his retirement as a medical examiner in a recruiting office. He inspected my left hand closely. The circular saw had cut across the back of the knuckles and had then licked the base of my upturned fingers as my hand had been whirled round for a fraction of a second. The scars lividly described the injury.

His stethoscope explored my chest and dwelt over my right lung. He paused in his examination and lowered the ear-pieces onto his shoulders. He seemed slightly perplexed.

"Have you ever had pneumonia?" he wondered aloud giving me a puzzled look.

"No, Doctor," I answered truthfully, fearful that he might next ask if I had ever been rejected by the Army on medical grounds.

He rubbed the side of his pockmarked nose with an ear-piece. With a sweeping look at me he completed his entries on a form and told me to get dressed and wait outside.

I sat in the outer office and waited. The sergeant was summoned into the doctor's surgery. Now alone, I became acutely conscious of myself and was eager to know if, at the third attempt, I had finally passed an Army medical examination. If not, I would, in desperation, try to enlist in the Tank Corps. Perversely, I wondered why I was here. Have I mortgaged my life for seven years? If so, what will Mam say when I tell her? My mind went blank.

The sergeant came out, his heavy tread vibrating the bare floorboards. He was holding a foolscap double form. He sat down, looking oddly out of place in his bright uniform behind a plain unpolished wooden desk. He wrote something on the form, my form. He stood up impressively to make his announcement.

"Right, lad, up you get – shoulders back. You're in the Army now!"

I ordered myself to smile.

CHAPTER 3

For many years recruits had been trained at Budbrooke Barracks. Now, the big barrack square no longer resounds to their heavy-booted feet as they respond to shouted orders. Military ghosts march silently through a new, executive-style housing estate that has arisen on the site of the razed barracks.

The barracks was a beehive of activity on 6 August 1938. That day I exchanged my civilian identity for a military one, when I became, after three attempts, Private Cottam of the Royal Warwickshire Regiment. I never regretted joining up, though it was physically costly. The Army would jolt me out of the apathy of an aimless life.

Sadly, the regiment, like its depot, has also perished. It was merged with some other doomed infantry units under a lumping new title that has "Fusiliers" woven into it in an attempt to quell disbelief and to claim respectability. Tribal loyalty was disregarded and tradition discounted so there are no soldiers these days with antelopes on their cap badges. George Bernard Shaw rightly observed in The Devil's Disciple that the British soldier can stand up to anything, except the British War Office.

I was put in the 1938 Peninsular Squad. The training squads were named repetitively after Battle Honours – Namur, South Africa, Vittoria (Len's), etc. – emblazoned on the regimental standard.

This newly-formed Peninsular Squad would not really have disheartened the training squad sergeant assigned to it when it 'paraded' before him for the first time. His assumed contempt for lowly recruits, expressed through theatrical asides, was part of the softening-up process as he set about moulding them into soldiers. In six month's time he would inherit yet another motley group of recruits, 'the worst lot I have ever clapped eyes on,' to lick into shape.

He walked slowly around us as we stood awkwardly, silently and nervously in a herded bunch. His penetrating eyes darting over us as if he was recalling when he himself had stood like us some twenty years previously. He was not merely smartly turned out, he shone with a glow that inspired awe and respect. Brass and leather gleaming. His pink cheeks had been scraped clean of audacious whiskers.

Completing a circuit, he again stood in front of us. We fidgeted and wondered what was coming next. He rolled his eyes heavenwards and pleaded: "Gawd, give me strength for the task that Thou has burdened me with."

Lowering his gaze he shouted: "Fall in, three ranks, tallest on the right!"

He began to whip his puttees with the heavy, silver-knobbed cane, which he would carry on drill sessions, as we shuffled into three ranks. Muttering among ourselves, we exchanged places on glancing over freshly cropped heads.

"Attention! Heels together, toes slightly apart, hands to sides, fingers curling inwards, thumbs to the front. Got that!"

Stiffly erect, he unclasped the big silver knob of his cane that now protruded from under an armpit, and demonstrated his requirements.

"When I command you to stand at ease, this is – Attention! I said *when!*"

We progressed slowly through the basic drill movements, marching with exaggerated swinging of arms, learning to keep in step, to wheel and to turn sharply in a body. Finally, we sagged to a "stand easy".

Relaxing a little himself the sergeant invited our reasons for joining the Army. In turn, we told him. Rouse, a big lad from

Coventry, opened for the defence. Our spokesman was dishonest and representative.

"Well, sir –"

"'Sergeant', always 'Sergeant' when you address me. Officers, second lieutenants and above, you will address as 'sir'," he interrupted, "others by their rank. I am your *Sergeant*," he concluded with a jutting chin and with a hint of an inverted superiority.

"Well – Sergeant, I expect to better myself. I had no prospects in my job as a factory hand..."

Generally, we all played safe, unimaginitively echoing Rouse when the metal tip of the cane was pointed accusingly at each of us in turn. Our compatible reasons for enlisting did not appear to astound him. He knew, and he knew we knew he knew, if you follow me, that most of us had simply drifted into the Army. It could have been the Navy or the Air Force. His questioning was therefore aimed at getting to know us, to see what he was up against, to identify potential trouble makers.

When our mumbling afterthoughts had dried up completely, the sergeant stiffened and said, "Right then, Now I shall tell you what the Army, and particularly this regiment, expects of you."

These expectations, which included our blind and total obedience as we were being moulded into images of our immediate superiors, were expressed robustly without faltering in a polished speech that he had delivered many times. The promised regime reminded me of my disciplined life in orphanages, where I had first learned the strategies of survival. I would again obey orders without questioning them beforehand, but this time I would be paid for my obedience.

Our sergeant seemed to mellow and to become almost friendly. "Tomorrow, he cajoled, "we shall begin arms drill with our new rifles, won't we? And, please, don't call them guns."

"I am now going to dismiss you – as you were! Get back in line!"

"On the command, *dismiss*, you will come to attention, smart right turn, then break ranks. Now – wait for the command."

He moved slowly along the length of his squad, scanning our expressionless faces. With a demonstrated, smartly executed about turn he marched back to a mid-position, halted, swivelled to face us and banged a raised boot down alongside the static one.

"When you get back to your barrack room, get changed for P.T. and report to the corporal in charge of the gym. You have five minutes to do that."

He gave us a last, lingering look and then bawled: "Dis-is-miss!"

We were a squad of thirty men whose ages ranging from the minimum of eighteen (the majority) to the maximum of twenty-five (Wildsmith). Wildsmith was actually thirty-five, admitting to twenty-five, and looking his real age because he was balding. It had been "agreed" discreetly with a recruiting officer that Wildsmith was not quite twenty-six. All of us were on the customary "seven and five", serving seven years with the colours and, on discharge, would serve five more years on reserve. An ex-soldier on reserve could be recalled for service should a national emergency arise and he would be instructed to "Keep yourself fit" on discharge from the colours.

On completion of seven year's service a soldier may be induced to serve an additional term. The completion of a pontoon, twenty-one years, would carry, along with its permanent imprint, a small pension.

After six months basic training at the Depot, and after successfully passing out, soldiers were sent to the home-based battalion. Peace-time county infantry regiments had two regular battalions, normally one home-based and the other stationed abroad. All other battalions of a regiment were usually territorial units.

Our 2nd. Battalion was stationed at Aldershot, the Mecca of the British Army. Our 1st. was on the N.W. frontier of India. Following the established pattern of alternating home and overseas postings the roles of the battalions would, eventually, be reversed. During this routine round of garrison postings at home and abroad the home-based unit would need to replenish the ranks of its remote sister battalion. The future destinations, therefore, of members of

Peninsular Squad were predictable: Aldershot and India. But this peaceful progression was going to be rudely interrupted by a war.

Our newly-formed squad was confined to barrack for the initial three weeks while ready-made khaki uniforms were being altered individually to fit us. We were not allowed to wear civvies and had only our fatigue uniforms that were made of a washable brown heavy linen. Fatigue dress was for barrack use only. When eventually we claimed our first issue of khaki we were allowed to venture outside the precincts of the barracks: on Saturday afternoons, if not on fatigues, and Sundays, after church parades.

The route out, in single file, lay through the Guard Room. The duty Guard-Room Commander would have to be satisfied that brass buttons and cap badge shone, and that brown hat strap was polished, white belt blancoed, puttees wrapped spirally from ankle to knee were at uniform spacings, black boots, which when issued had been dull and dimpled, were spit and circular polished until they resembled black mirrors and their brass lace eyelets polished. If a turn-out appeased the NCO: Dismiss! Retrieve Malacca silver-knobbed swagger cane tucked under arm and, with a self-conscious grin – out!

Our pay, as recruits, was two shillings a day – fourteen shillings (70p) a week. On Friday mornings we marched in turn up to a desk behind which sat the pay officer and saluted him for some, not all, of it. Saving a part of pay was compulsory. My gross weekly pay had been already reduced to nine shillings (45p) because I had allocated five shillings (25p) of it to my mother. This was in case anything should happen to me while soldiering. If the worst thing possible did, then Mam, being a widow, might become eligible for a pension from the Army.

We spent hours 'square bashing'. The instructions: "Up two three, down two three," along with other advice, would remain with us for ever.

"Fix your bayonet firmly or it may land point first on the man behind as you shoulder arms."

"Only foreign soldiers click their heels when they spring to attention."

"Don't bang your rifle butt on the ground when ordering arms,"

It was essential that the drill movements of recruits were absolutely synchronised for its squad to pass out on completion of basic training. There was no 'if' about a squad's ability to pass out, only 'when', even if it took a consecutive six months of more intensive training.

Finally, an immaculately turned out squad of recruits was drilled as if it were replicas of one man. The lone squad on the vast barrack square then remained at attention, rifles at the 'slope', and hoped the inspecting depot commander would salute in acknowledgement.

Our first training-squad sergeant, beneath his parade-ground exterior, was a kind, caring man. Off duty he was surprisingly self-effacing and withdrawn. His successor was a husky-voiced, characteristic type of warrant officer who sinisterly confided: "You play ball wiv me, an' I'll play ball wiv you." He was difficult to love and it was his ball.

Afternoon school came as a welcome respite from physical training and field training, even though the overweight Royal Army Education Corps sergeant made us wistfully aware that we ought to have paid more attention to our previous teachers. The men in the squad were almost all from working class homes and were elementary school educated. The exceptions were Mahon, a wiry Irishman, and Evans, a big, rugged Welshman. Both had been to public schools.

Len's squad passed out and was granted a furlough before being sent to Aldershot. My interim awarded leave coincided with his final one so we travelled to Birmingham together. Mam beamed with pride on seeing the transformation wrought by the Army in her biggest son.

"My, you've grown. But what have you done to your hair?" It was kept short and had been flattened regularly with a sharp rimmed tin helmet or a peaked hat.

As ordained, when Peninsular Squad passed out it also was dispatched to Aldershot. A section of the battalion Drums met the squad at Farnborough Station and escorted it on the short march to

Ramillies Barracks. We marched behind the fife players. The jaunty drummers led the way, rhythmically accompanying the stirring martial music. With sloped arms we marched, self-consciously at first then proudly, behind swinging, brightly polished bugles that were low-slung on lanyards hanging from the shoulders of all our escorts, drummers and musicians alike.

The squad was swallowed by 'D' Company and considerately kept together in a newly formed platoon. Being with comrades, with whom we had spent an impressionable six months, helped us to find our feet in a strangely magnified military environment where everyone in and around the many separated barracks was invisibly dressed in khaki or fatigues. A woman, particularly if in civilian clothes, would have stopped the military traffic. Aldershot was then approaching the peak of its military population.

I did not see much of Len while we were in Ramillies Barracks. Our training programmes differed in times or venues, he being in 'C' Company. We did manage to meet a few times at the Garrison Cinema.

Len was inoculated against some fatal tropical diseases. After a permitted spell of excused duty to recuperate from the after-affects of the jabs, he and his batch were ready for a long sea voyage to India.

We split up after a late show at the cinema. As we shared out our remaining cigarettes I noticed that Len seemed downcast. Subdued and downcast, perhaps realising that we had lost control of our destinies. "Hope you hit it off with my sister, mate," were his parting words to me.

Len then followed the route taken by his many brothers. I was not to follow Len this time.

Our training became ominously more intensive. The battalion joined the Brigade (5th.), the rest of the Division (2nd.Infantry) and the entire Army Corps (1st.), so it was said, when out on manoeuvres. Those in the ranks would not 'see' beyond even their own company when on long arduous route marches – sometimes 'forced' through the night and always in full pack – over exhausting territory.

Mechanised transport in the battalion was restricted to a small number of military versions of the Austin Seven car and some motor bikes for dispatch riders. The little Austins were going to be replaced by canvas-covered trucks, eight hundredweight P.U.s with low-pressure balloon tyres and fifteen hundredweights with bullet-proof tyres.

M.T. Platoon H.Q. Company, would require extra drivers for this greater number of vehicles that would allow some of the men as well as all heavy equipment to be moved independently by the battalion's own transport. Evans and I anticipated this. Goaded by a mutual dislike of thirsty, blistering route marches, we both applied for a company transfer and to be trained as truck drivers. "If we have to patrol the surrounding countryside, let's do so on wheels," Taff suggested in his sing-song voice.

After being trained, I enjoyed manoeuvres, tearing around the countryside, charging through bracken and brambles and skewing along ploughed fields. The tractor-type treads of the solid, bullet-proof tyres on my new fifteen hundredweight truck enabled it to climb the steepest and muddiest of inclines.

Surprisingly, Taff had failed to pass out as a truck driver. He had no mechanical aptitude, he was told. He had an aptitude for figures, though, and he wangled a transfer to the Pay Corps to use this ability.

When I was doing a turn as duty driver I had occasionally to deliver packages to the original Glasshouse. The North Camp prison owed its name to its glass roof. The name afterwards spread to refer to all military prisons. Whereas our 'jankers' included doubling round the barrack square in full pack, prisoners in the Glasshouse did everything at the double, from reveille, which officially started another Army day, until lights out. To the cookhouse, to fatigues, to parades, to and from everywhere they doubled in squads flanked by bellowing NCOs. When weaving a way through columns criss-crossing the barrack square, I would feel sorry for the poor sods.

Outside those uninviting gates we also were strictly disciplined – on the parade ground it was of the iron variety – but not unrelentingly as those were inside them.

Inspections on our Adjutant's Parades were extremely thorough and carried out to the minutist detail on a soldier who had been randomly selected. An unlucky specimen was rarely deemed perfectly turned out. A speck of dust that had escaped being pulled through and out of a rifle barrel by four by two material, or a removed bolt not revealing a slight smear of oil from the bottle carried in the brass butt along with the corded pull through, would result in the victim shouting: "Name, rank, number, Sah!" The hovering R.S.M. would then lick his poised indelible pencil before it descended inexorably to a note-pad.

On company parades we learned, sometimes the hard way, that one officer was afflicted with an unnerving mannerism, and he seemed to be oblivious of it. When talking, or rather ordering, as far as we in the ranks were concerned, he would frame his speech with swift, unexpected smiles. His mouth would elongate momentarily then shrink suddenly and the short-lived smile would vanish. This facial distortion would flash on and off like a neon sign. Flash. "Get your hair cut. Take his name, Sergeant-Major!" Flash.

Passing along the ranks, pausing briefly to adjust the hat of an unresisting rigid soldier, he could unwittingly induce a new man to smile back at him – companionably. That costly reflex action would be construed as getting insolently familiar with an officer for 'Smiler' had not really been expressing his joy at seeing him. Too late, the new man would realise that he should have ignored that involuntary smile on the officer's face, but the damage would have been done.

Along with other recent innovations, such as the abandonment of the system of marching to meals, the military crime of 'dumb insolence', the last resort of hapless officers, had been abolished. So, to maintain the proper standards of disciplined behaviour on the parade ground, Smiler would persevere with a personal inspection until he found something else about the grinning imbecile facing him that was bookable. It was never a difficult task.

"Disgraceful! Put this man on a charge, Sergeant-Major!" he

39

would scream between flashes. Another novitiate, while relieved of his spare time for a regulation number of days, would take the vow not to repeat the blunder.

A ceremonial parade, to honour the sovereign's birthday, for example, held more perils for majorities than for individuals since it involved precise movements of a great number of men. Whole platoons, companies even, would be at risk of being confined to barracks for extra, prolonged drill sessions.

I began to wonder what was the point of it all? An officer would explain that thousands of men in a garrison town have to be tightly controlled and fully occupied, even though some of their repetitive duties might seem purposeless, otherwise a disciplined army might degenerate quickly into a rabble. And that wouldn't do, old chap, would it?

CHAPTER 4

One cool sunny morning in the spring of '39, the whole battalion clustered loosely around the perimeter of the vast barrack square and waited patiently to assemble on it for an important ceremonial parade. The leading side drummer, with upraised sticks in a horizontal straight line under his nostrils, stood alone on the grey tarmac. Without any shouted orders, obeying just single drum taps, we came to attention, marched to our stations, fell-in, right dressed and remained at attention. The CO, through his RSM, then took control.

Two opposite sides of the parade ground were lined with long, three deep ranks of soldiers in markedly separated companies. The faces of all the rigid soldiers had the same blank expressions, their eyes staring across the square at other blank faces. Officers, who fronted them, had similarly been frozen to statues. At the top of the parade ground, positioned between the opposed companies, the regimental band stood behind the corps of drums. Facing the drums, at the bottom of the parade ground and completing the inward-looking square formation – the Colonel. Resplendent, stiffly proud, he was astride his white charger. His basket-hilted sword was held firmly and threateningly, pointing downwards as if ready to cleave an imaginary foe, a ground-based inferior.

Polished brass gleamed and burnished steel shone. Cherry black leather, chestnut brown leather and snow white leather complemented bright metal. The 2nd. Battalion of the Royal Warwickshire Regiment was on full ceremonial parade. It must have been an impressive sight, even to traditionally critical neighbours in adjacent barracks.

In front of the Drum Major, facing the distanced Colonel, stood our richly decorated regimental mascot, an antelope, officially named 'Bobby', but unofficially and affectionately known to us in the ranks as Billy the Kid. He was draped with an embroidered saddle cloth.

Billy had posed, and was now poised, between two drummer boys who held him captive on two separate long reins. These white-blancoed reins were attached to bright metal rings that sprouted from opposite sides of the mascot's white-blancoed collar. Already the slack had been taken up in the reins. The ante-lope was visibly shaking. The restraining drummer boys, whose dreaded turns had come round again to "volunteer" for the privileged roles in a ceremonial parade, were wise to the predictable, but no doubt fearful of the unpredictable, antics of their charge. They might even have had a foreboding that it was not going to be their day.

The ornate silver tips (nice touch, this) on the tops of the antelope's slowly twisting, tapering horns flashed in the strengthening sunlight as his head jerked. The reins held in young, white-gloved, opposite hands began to tension ominously, forcing the boys to step sideways towards each other and to arrow our trembling mascot. The fresh faces of the handlers now registered apprehension in case Billy decided suddenly to take a look up the nose of that much bigger and strangely still quadruped several yards away that seemed to be staring at him.

Everyone else on parade was perfectly still. We were all tuned in to the Regimental Sergeant Major who would give the next command.

When he gave the command: "SLOW – OH – PARMS!" Bobby, alias Billy, made a bolt for it. With one tremendous forward leap the deserting antelope disengaged itself from its handlers and off it shot, flailing reins trailing.

Antelopes can shift. They depend on an almost instant maximum acceleration in their natural habitat to escape from predators. At a quick rearward glance, the visible parts of the big-bass drummer's leopard-skin apron could have been mistaken for a stalking big cat, which also can go at a fair lick, particularly before an anticipated lunch. Antelopes are instinctively aware of this. That is why there are still some left in Africa.

Our steadfast Colonel, ready to salute his men in acknowledgement, was now holding his sword in the upright position, forearm stiffly and dramatically horizontal. Only he could bar the antelope's path to freedom. His horse reared up and it seemed we were about to have two regimental mascots when the whole one dashed under his sword. The Colonel's pink face registered fury then dismay while we found it hard to retain our expressionless looks...

After the parade, while releasing our pent-up mirth, we were told that the Colonel had felt quite sharp about this impromptu item in the morning's programme, although the rampant antelope had not got very far before it was recaptured. Dutifully, our officers had not been amused, either.

Our humourless officers were strict disciplinarians. We had to accept their authority and we respected them. Some of them we even liked. When off duty, they did not associate with other ranks. The officers' mess was out of bounds to everyone below the rank of second lieutenant. Non-commissioned officers, sergeant-majors and sergeants, were just as strict with those beneath them and were segregated socially from both the groups they separated. Traditionally, even an officer could not enter the sergeants' mess without an invitation. While officers and noncoms were free to visit the lower ranks' canteen, they rarely intruded on our privacy. We all knew our places in the military community, particularly when not on duty.

However, as the tattoo approached, our officers became embarrassingly chummy towards us. They needed our *voluntary* co-operation when we were off duty.

To achieve Cecil B. DeMille panoramas, great numbers of soldiers were needed for an Aldershot Tattoo, an annual outdoor event staged on consecutive nights in aid of a military charity. It was the custom to inveigle the lowest ranks in the garrison town to volunteer for the big crowd scenes, and apparently our CO had already generously 'offered' our block services, leaving it to his officers to find and donate their quotas of men.

I was ordered to report to my MT Platoon officer. The lieutenant's office led off the big garage that housed the trucks. I knocked on the opened door.

"Enter!"

The young lieutenant looked up from his cluttered desk. "Congratulations, Cottam! You did well on the firing range last week. So well, in fact, that you are wanted back in 'D' Company to train as a sniper. Does that please you?"

It didn't. In future my excellent marksmanship on the rifle range would mysteriously deteriorate. "I don't think I would like to be a sniper, sir. It is a lonely and dangerous job when on active service, which doesn't seem to be far off."

"I must point out that a trained sniper would earn proficiency pay."

"For how long?" He raised his eyebrows in silent mirth and suppressed a smile.

"I take it then you are not keen on the idea?"

"I'd prefer sit in a truck with others than sit alone in the fork of a tree – sir." He smiled.

"Okay. I am prepared to say I cannot afford to lose another driver since we are already short of them."

"Are we, sir?"

"No, and your not indispensable. But I am prepared to say you are." He leaned back in his comfortable chair and openly grinned at me. "Now, since I am willing to help you," he said. "I would like you to help me." He was looking directly at me. I began to smell a large rodent.

"I am having difficulty in making up the platoon's quota of men for the tattoo. Will you volunteer? And will you encourage some of the other drivers to do likewise?" His eyebrows were raised expectantly as he waited for the only acceptable answer.

"Er – yes, sir."

"Good man. I'll see to it that you won't have to climb trees. Quid pro quo."

"Sir?"

"A favour returned – dismiss!"

As we were naturally disadvantaged, our NCOs came along to look after us when treacherously we had 'volunteered' to take part in the tattoo. But, for a change, we led the way.

Volunteers in the ranks of our H.Q. Company acted as torch bearers in one gigantic scene and as Elizabethan pikemen in another. We spent hours of our off-duty time, late afternoons to dark evenings, rehearsing complex drill sequences aided by white tapes laid on the turf.

As torch bearers we wore a colourful uniform of an infantry soldier of bygone days, red tunic, white belt, black trousers with a wide red stripe down the seams and a kind of policeman's helmet. At least, it was a change from dull khaki.

We were distributed uniformly among the massed bands. We marched, in a huge square formation, in quick time, in slow time, reverting to quick time. Up and down, across, diagonally, over springy turf that released an earthy aroma from beneath our crushing boots, With the floodlighting switched off, our held-high naphtha torches formed geometrical patterns of moving light and gave just enough illumination for the bandsmen to read their sheet music. Finally, we wheeled and marched directly up to the rostrum on which stood the conductor who was waving at us with his illuminated baton.

I had been positioned at the end of a line and had been given a scowling Coldstream Guards corporal to bathe with mellow light from my wandering torch. He played a clarinet, which had a very small sheet of music stuck on its end. He looked down at me contemptuously and had made it quite clear that if I allowed just one teeny drop of flaming oil to land from my hissing flare onto his lovely black bearskin, he would ram my torch vertically upwards so that its smoke came out of my ears. I trod warily while marching over the uneven turf. Guardsmen are big blokes. Mine would have towered over me even if he had stood in a hole.

The pipers and drummers of the Scots Guards and Highland Regiments were also fiercely impressive in their kilted dress uniforms, with jewel knobbed dirks hanging from their belts and amber-headed skein dhus thrust down the tops of their stockings. I liked their bagpipe music, even though it started up with a moan.

The pikemen in the Elizabethan scene were arranged in two long rows, three or four deep, for a grand finale. We had to greet Queen Elizabeth who, perched on a white horse, rode slowly between the rows.

We were dressed in shades of blue: dark blue doublets, striped blue ballooning knickerbockers and pale blue hose. Incongruously, as a closer inspection would have revealed, we wore our own black ammunition boots with their tops turned down. We were armed with pikes, which were sixteen feet (five metres) long, and wore breastplates. The breastplates and the spearheads of our pikes were made of silvered cardboard. We were warned not to jab one another playfully with our weapons because a folded spearhead destroyed realism.

As our beloved Queen Elizabeth rode into view, those of us in the front ranks were ordered to bow and lower our pikes in salute: "Spontaneously, not simultaneously, if you please!" Shades of HMS Pinafore!

Permitted this random freedom of expression, some of the pikemen sank on one knee and wailed uncontrollably. We all cheered loyally as the Queen, a deliberately anonymous RAMC corporal, who was dressed in a white robe and a flowing blonde wig, and who sat side-saddle on a white horse, inspected her troops. The bawled, repeated questions (the politest being: "Who's taking you home tonight, dearie?") were muted and edited to expressions of love for our Virgin Queen when they reached a distant audience.

The performances finished late in the evenings. Before being transported back to barracks, we were served with a hot meal in the big marquees, which had been specially erected for this purpose, and given a few coppers, enough to buy a small packet of cigarettes. Our orderly officers did their best to make our extended working days bearable.

One night, someone mistook my silk stockings for their's and I was rejected as an incompletely dressed performer. Outcast, I sat on a grassy knoll overlooking the arena. Knickerbockered, bare-legged but booted, I leaned against the trunk of a big tree, which had exposed, fingering roots grabbing at the earth. I saw the rest of the performance from my lone vantage point. The music swelled and fell gently in the velvety cool night breeze that softly rustled the leaves above my head. It was a wonderful spectacle, a superb display of soldierly precision. I forgave whoever had pinched my stockings.

That Aldershot Tattoo and its smaller rival, the Tidworth Tattoo, put on in 1939 were the last of the tattoos before the outbreak of a war. The calendar of military pageantry would be adjourned while new material for it accumulated.

We returned to our normal pre-tattoo barrack routine and I was ready for a new challenge when the Army extended the scope of the Bren machine gun by providing an armoured conveyance for it – the Bren-gun Carrier. As with the allocation of trucks, there was a shortage of drivers for the ten new vehicles. Covetting a pair of carrier driver's goggles, I joined the newly formed Carrier Platoon.

Imagine a light tank with the top cut off. That then, basically, would be a carrier, an open type of armour plated tracked vehicle with a front turret mounting for the adaptable Bren gun. Power was supplied by a rear-mounted Ford V8 engine that was fed by twin, twenty gallon petrol tanks. The high-revving engine was coupled to a crash gearbox that demanded double-de-clutching for noise-less gear changes. Top whack was about 60 m.p.h. At that maximum, screaming speed, with the engine noise level loud enough to crack teeth, steering, braking and gear changing demanded great care to retain control of a maverick steed.

The gunner sat next to the driver. The third member of the crew sat behind the gunner. The cubicle behind the driver contained a tarpaulin, tools, machete in a leather scabbard and a Boys anti-tank rifle. Hand grenades, when issued, would nestle sinisterly in cushioned steel boxes. Ammunition would have to be stuffed somewhere, .303 bullets for the Bren gun and the three Lee-

Enfields, .55 armour-piercing bullets for the a/t rifle.

The anti-tank rifle was developed by the German Army in the Great War, after the British had invented the tank (a curious boast), its target. Our powerful rifle, which had the kick of a mule, would prove to be an inadequate weapon when used against modern heavy tanks. Also, the flash eliminator, on the end of the long barrel, could fail to conceal the rifle's whereabouts, and so would attract an explosive reply to a presumption.

The Bren-gun Carrier was a nippy, lively vehicle with the climbing ability of a mountain goat, but it would be handicapped in certain active service terrains. Because of its open top it would be vulnerable to having nasty things dropped into it from bedroom windows when patrolling suburban streets. No doubt, it would be an ideal fighting machine in open country, particularly in a desert where, I am reliably told, there are no trees and therefore no enemies likely to be lurking up any.

The function, in war, of Carrier Platoon would be to spearhead the advance of the battalion when things were going well, and to cover its retreat when they were not. Everyone would know where to find Carrier Platoon. In peace-time it was jocularly known in the battalion as the Suicide Squad. We used to laugh at that – then.

It was exciting fighting pre-arranged 'battles' when training, swathing paths through woods, clattering through quiet villages, tearing at speed across fields, practising ditch jumping. Issued with blank cartridges for our rifles and armed with pickaxe handles we skirmished with 'enemies' on night-time exercises. We were advised not to use the metal end of a pickaxe handle on an opponent's head, unless it was protected with a tin helmet.

The close group of ten drivers formed the core of Carrier Platoon. We were a varied lot and comradely: Poulton, a muscular, quiet, grave-looking man; Philpots (Phil), his very opposite, slim and jokey; Killeen (Killer), lanky, ever exuberant; Clancy, slight of build and a flamboyant extrovert; Mathews (Mat), stiffly built, a dour reservist, who before his recall drove a London bus...

I was dubbed Cush (easy going). Our likeable platoon sergeant was known, off parade, simply as 'H'. The platoon officer,

Lieutenant Lynn-Allen, who was both respected and liked, was dutifully and sincerely called 'Sir'.

The gunners of our carriers were primarily drummers and fife players, normally under the command of a drum major. Similarly, they seemed to be just as close-knit under their commander. They joined us only occasionally for their ceremonial duties limited the time they could spend in their token jobs in Carrier Platoon. In peace time we saw little of them. Their dual military roles were about to be merged into the unmusical one, and carrier drivers would then acquire permanent crews.

We were recalled from manoeuvres a week before war was declared. In the mad rush back to barracks I collided with a fifteen hundredweight truck being driven frantically in the opposite direction. The Manchester Regiment driver was unhurt but his vehicle had suffered.

The battalion was strictly confined to barracks. On a sunny Sunday morning, at fifteen minutes past eleven, Prime Minister Neville Chamberlain, solemnly addressed the nation.

In his reedy tones he announced that: "... this country is now at war with Germany."

As did their fathers on the outbreak of the Great War, the younger, optimistic members of Carrier Platoon thought it would all be over by Christmas.

CHAPTER 5

Just after the declaration of war, the battalion moved out of Aldershot. The main body embarked at Southampton. MT Platoon and Carrier Platoon (without the gunners) joined a long convoy that headed west, winding its unsignposted way round anonymous towns. Our secret destination proved to be Newport, Monmouthshire, as it was. Only one of our battalion's vehicles failed to reach the embarkation port.

Near Newport I 'ran' a big end. I was ordered to garage my sick carrier at the back of a country pub. While waiting for further instructions, I sat in the public bar. No, I did not know where we were going. Privately, I thought we might be going to France since an unexpected turn of garrison duty in Palestine had suddenly been cancelled and our recent incapacitating inoculations had not included those against tropical diseases.

"Honestly, I don't know where we'll disembark. Like you, I can only guess." That frank admission went down well. I was in. "That's very kind of you. Cheers!"

A warrant officer from another unit rolled up in a truck and spoiled my evening by extricating me from the bar. He then ordered me to salvage the tools from the immobilised carrier and wrap them in the big tarpaulin that was used to cover the vehicle when it was stationary in wet weather.

"The tools will be going with you," he said. "They'll be needed for the replacement carrier that will be sent out to your battalion."

"Won't it be supplied with a tool kit?" I complained. It was daunting being lumbered with, and held responsible for, a heavy load of ironmongery on a sea trip to goodness knows where. Heedless of my bleating, the efficient warrant officer commandeered the Bren gun and the Boys anti-tank rifle. My rifle remained with me – unfortunately, as it turned out. No ammunition had been issued.

The troops due for an imminent sea voyage were bivouacked in long rows in a big field. There were hundreds of drivers. Parked nearby were their tanks, carriers, trucks and towed artillery pieces. Separated from our units, we would disembark at a different port, presumably one that had quick-unloading facilities for a great number of vehicles.

We embarked next day at Newport Docks. With some help I managed to stash my heavy tool kit in the hold of the requisitioned cargo ship, and then I clambered up narrow steel staircases, which linked the congested, stiflingly hot decks, and reached heavenly fresh air. The only available space left for a latecomer to kip down was on the top deck. The gently throbbing ship was now crammed with drivers and their personal equipment.

We sailed before dusk. The landfall began to extend astern, then it faded.

I awoke early. My body was stiff through lying on a hard deck that vibrated gently with the rhythmic pulse of the ship's engines. Following a chilly night, the morning was a perfection of blue haze and sea mist. Soon, it became warm, balmy with a clear blue sky. We were alone on the sparkling high seas except for a Royal Navy escorting destroyer that had appeared suddenly to disturb the almost flat, calm seascape with its wake. The warship zig-zagged across our bows on long, curving tacks at astonishing speed and agility, cutting the water cleanly.

There came the first stirrings of a slow sea breeze. Waves began to lap gently against the sides of the ship. Gulls, crying mournfully, overtook us with effortless ease, planing and swooping above the creaming waves. On that lovely sunny day it was hard to imagine that men were making preparations to kill each other, that the ship would be a prime target for a U-boat.

I went below and queued to get washed. I managed to get a quick wash, but was jostled out of my turn for a shave, so I didn't bother. The eagle-eyed Army officer, i/c all troops on board ship, spotted the omission as soon as I had climbed up onto the top deck.

"Get shaved!" he barked at me.

"It's taken me an hour to just wash – sir!" I said with the fierceness of a man trying to control himself.

"Go back down and shave," he ordered me, "even if it takes you another hour."

"Kinell!" I said under my breath.

There was a perceptible swell with a light variable wind as we steamed across the Bay of Biscay and into the considerable landing port of St. Nazaire. The tigerish escort departed as swiftly as it had arrived and our ship continued to sail, very slowly, up the River Loire, the longest river in France, my geography told me. It was lit up in the still bright sun. We reached Nantes and the ship berthed tightly – with difficulty, it seemed.

We had made a good crossing. The battalion's crossing to Cherbourg was recorded officially as rough. It is not recorded officially that MT and Carrier Platoons of its HQ Company had been transported on a separate, longer route.

The inhabitants packing the high quayside in the late afternoon looked directly across the ship's crowded top deck. They cheered us lustily. There was a carnival atmosphere under a setting sun that glowed benignly.

We marched into the city and slept that night in an old cinema that had had its auditorium stripped of serried rows of seats in readiness for military patrons. The drivers of Carrier Platoon stuck together in the midst of hundreds of sprawling men.

Next morning, when retrieving my tool kit from the bowels of the dirty cargo vessel, I noticed that our Royal Engineers were manning the tall dockside cranes. They were unloading the ships that had transported the heavier equipment. The battalion's carriers, along with all other tracked vehicles, were not handed over to their respective drivers. To conserve their tracks, they would be sent by rail to final destinations rather than be driven long distances on metalled roads.

The battalion's carrier drivers boarded a train and I joined them, a little breathlessly, after stowing my tool kit in a rear van. A great sadness edged with fear swept over me. In the general confusion, and in my anxiety to get my tools entrained safely, I had lost my rifle. It was stolen when, trustingly, I had propped it against a stanchion while manhandling the tarpaulin covered bulk. The rifle was in its special canvas case that had no sling so it could not be slung over a shoulder. Off the parade ground I had always kept that meticulously cleaned, bolt-action Lee-Enfield in its case. My rifle had served me well when competing on the range. Now it had been nicked by some thieving swine.

Losing a rifle was a court-martial offence. That fact of military life let loose my imagination. The trial in time of war round an upturned drum for summary judgement is known as a Drumhead Court Martial. Undeniably guilty, what would be my fate?

Everyone in our packed compartment sympathised with me: first his carrier, and now his *bondook*.The platoon sergeant said he would try and get my tool kit transported officially to wherever we were going, just in case, as he wryly put it: "You're three times unlucky."

Sergeant North, 'H', was dark-skinned, smoothfaced and in his early thirties. Slightly overweight, he was not your standard Army sergeant. He was more mechanic than soldier. A thoughtful, studious man he was quietly authoritative. He was so liked by his drivers that he hardly ever needed to pull rank to maintain discipline in the platoon.

The train puffed and fussed out of the station and, after a short journey, rumbled into another. French rolling stock seemed to be mounted on square wheels.

We were not allowed off the train, so this was not to be our temporary destination. I noticed that the platform was crowded with swirling people. Most of them were in uniform and the British Army was well represented.

There came a knock on the carriage door. Clancy, the nearest one to the strap, lowered the window. My old MT Platoon officer thrust a rifle through the opening and shouted at us: "Tell Cottam to look after that!"

It would have been indiscreet to ask where he had "found" a rifle. Relieved, I fell asleep and dreamt that the enterprising young officer, who again had got me off the hook, had located a surplus Bren-gun carrier to replace the one left at the back of a pub near Newport.

We camped in the grounds of an old chateau, on the outskirts of Le Mans. Here we were re-united with our battalion.

A convenient high-banked stream flowing gently through the park land provided us with the means to wash and bathe. Wherever we were sent, however spartan our accommodation, high standards of hygiene would be maintained. Regular personal inspections would be carried out to ensure this. Diseases such as cholera and typhoid, which could march with an army and rage through a body of troops like a rampant plague, were thus kept at bay.

Later, in Belgium, when given a rare opportunity, we would cut off the tops of 5-gallon petrol tins and boil our underclothes in them over a wood fire. It was advisable to wear clean underclothes before going into battle to contain infection if wounded.

The battalion moved up in stages to the French and Belgian border in the northern industrial area of France. We travelled in RASC trucks.

Grouped in companies, we were billeted in and around Rumegies and alternated duties there with those at extreme posts. The border country was flat, featureless, unadorned by trees and cross-cut by canals and drainage ditches.

The BEF, in which our division and the 1st. were the only fully trained troops, had been assigned the task of defending this sector. One did not have to be a military genius in the Marlborough class to be able to predict that the inevitable German offensive would most likely be directed through Belgium. If the attack was not long delayed, it would be met by a much thinner 'thin red line' than the one met in the Great War.

Our platoon was lodged in a small relinquished terraced house on the edge of Rumegies village. Our new home had been uninvitingly emptied of all its furniture. Every room, up and down, was used as sleeping quarters. We slept, six or seven to a room, on thin palliasses on bare wooden floors. I pencilled reminder notices to myself on my wall space. Phil, on the adjacent palliasse, drew a naked woman, exaggerating his physical preferences. "To remind myself what I'm missing," he explained.

I took delivery of my new carrier and accustomed myself to driving it on the "wrong" side of the road. The replacement was a Scout Carrier, as used by the Royal Artillery for observation purposes. Designated as a non-combatant vehicle ('Mild steel only, no armour plate') it was not even equipped with a turret mounting for a Bren gun.

It was difficult to fire a mounted Bren as the carrier, bobbing and weaving, sped over rough country. It would be impossible to fire a hand-held machine gun while on the move. When this carrier was stationary, the agile gunner would be at risk of exposure if forced to use an improvised support for his weapon, and all the crew would be protected by inferior steel.

I garaged my carrier in a farmer's ramshackle yard barn and became friendly with his spinster daughter. She began to correspond, in her native language, with my mother since my own letters home were censored. Later, our letters home were heavily censored. Even the embroidered greetings cards, the so-called 'silk cards', which were more prolific in the Great War, could not escape selective obliterations. We were then restricted to field postcards that had to have the inappropriate sentences printed on them deleted by the sender. A recipient of them would glean only that the sender was still living and that he could draw parallel lines reasonably straight, freehand. Marie with her dignified French kept my mother better informed about my welfare.

During the battalion's Armistice Day parade on 11 November 1939 the alarm was raised that Germany was about to invade Holland and Belgium. The parade was instantly dismissed and we were ordered to prepare for an immediate move northwards.

I ran to the barn and quickly refilled the twinned petrol tanks of my carrier before – instead of after – reversing it out of the darkened rickety building. Very fortunately, I had promptly replaced both tank caps. To check the engine oil level in that poor light I foolishly lit a match, forgetting in my haste that the floor pan might be awash with spilled petrol. It was.

A flash of bright light merged with a minor explosion. I dived over the back of the carrier and almost collided with the little old farmer who had come running towards me on bandy legs. He had not hurried to see if I was hurt. His anxiety for the state of his barn was plainly written on his flushed, animated face. He yelled abuse at me at an untranslatable speed. Two other carrier drivers, Killer and Clancy, who were just passing the farm entrance, grabbed their fire extinguishers and put out the fire.

"Are you burned, Cush?" asked Killer anxiously.

"My eyebrows are singed, but that's all – I think."

Apart from some blistering of new paint, my carrier was undamaged. Old wooden supports of the barn had been slightly scorched and some straw had been reduced to ashes and that, luckily, was the full extent of the damage done.

Mollified a little as the smoke cleared in wisps, the farmer became less voluble. In a quieter voice he asked me why had I filled up in the barn instead of out in the yard. He asked me in faltering English mixed with rapid French. In hesitant colloquial French, interjected with forceful English, I pointed out that I would have done if I hadn't been in a hurry and if that bloody great farm cart, which had blocked my exit, had been moved straight away.

In stooping to reach for the oil-level dipstick I had received the blast of flame in my face, which had not only sizzled my hair and removed my eyebrows but had, I now discovered, blistered my cheeks. After my face had been larded with a soothing cream by the MO's orderly the alarm, which had been raised with such believable irony on that Remembrance Day, proved to be false. We were stood down.

I showed my face daily to the MO for examination. A week later he discharged me as fit: medicine and duty. The next day, on HQ Company parade, Major Hicks stared at my hideously scabbed face, shuddered, and sent me straight back to the MO. "And tell him I sent you!" he commanded.

I was now seriously worried about being left with permanent facial scars. Gratefully, I was not. Marie considerately forgot to mention the incident in her next letter to my mother, who was assured that I was keeping well.

Our festive dinner on Christmas Day 1939 was held in a local community hall. In view of the numbers, we dined on a company rota basis. Ritually, the officers served their men before leaving for their own meal. A cabaret star, Frances Day, entertained some of the soldiers in the area.

While we were stationed at Rumeges King George arrived to see his troops, and the town was also visited by many celebrities including the Duke of Gloucester, Neville Chamberlain and Noel Coward. Unsociably, we along with most others in the ranks, were never in when our famous visitors called to see us. We were always out in working parties.

Every available man in the battalion worked daily along a section of the 40-mile stretch of silent frontier allotted to the BEF. We had been laying concrete foundations for pillboxes. When it became much too cold to lay concrete we excavated earth to form massive tank traps, earth sloped down to abrupt walls, stabbing at the frozen, iron-hard crust with picks before using spades. The exposed deep walls of the traps were shored up with vertical pine poles rammed home with the aid of gigantic two-man mallets. Typically a makeshift 'mallet' was a length of telegraph pole, tipped with iron and having two long grab handles like ears, each of which would be shared by two opposing up and downers.

Our platoon picked and shovelled, except Poulton and H, who for once pulled rank: "Every working gang needs a good foreman," he maintained with a triumphant grin.

The muscular Poulton stared over top of a mallet at a brawny, red-haired Jock, who called the hefty pine poles wee cabers. "Every time we come down with the mallet," Poulton said when we were having a short break, "Big Mac's kilt wafts up!"

"Is he wearing anything under it?" we were curious to know.

"He is now! The icy weather must have got up there," Poulton grinned as he tipped out the dregs of tea from his small mess tin and folded its handle before encasing it in the big tin. As he put them away in his small pack Mat asked him: "The big Jock on the next mallet has a bandaged knee. What happened?"

"That's Dick. Top of a pole broke off as they were hammering it home. He's a fiery bugger, effing and blinding all the time, so don't call him Big otherwise you'll end up propping up the bank between two poles and with a flat head."

Our sergeant eased his comfortable frame off a stack of odd sized poles that he had been allocating and joined his gang. "Shovel out what you've broken up and we'll call it a day. Poulton, get back to Big Mac. He wants to ram in one last pole."

Months later, when the Germans made their belated two-pronged attack, the Belgium prong must have paused to admire our workmanship. Then, unsportingly ignoring the rules, it bypassed the tank traps.

Throughout January and February the hard winter held the future battlefield in its relentless iron grip. Traditionally, BEF played for time in those months until an effective fighting force had been built up and a defence system constructed. Meanwhile, the threat of an imminent German attack through the Netherlands began obligingly to recede.

The endless winter seemed to have frozen time itself. Leaden, immense skys over the flat land contributed to make our tasks seem eternal. Keen winds sweeping from far horizons cut like knives as we laboured on those cheerless, cold-blast days with cold-bitten ears and watering eyes. The desolate scenery was enhanced a little by the seas of snow that hid all details and smoothed out the few angles, but our dispiriting, uneventful days were as dull and drab as the khaki fatigue kilts worn by the labouring Jocks.

Guard duties, two on and four off round the clock, were particularly loathed in the icy weather. We fortified ourselves against the numbing cold with rum when on stag during the night. The beers of the wine-loving country were in the main about as potent as shandy. No wonder French children were allowed to drink the weak brews. None of us, however, were in a tremendous hurry to sample the renowned and superior German beers.

During this so called 'phony war' period the battalion kept providing the RE's with working parties. We began to feel that the BEF alone was having to extend, if roughly, the Maginot Line from Montmedy to the coast, to where, logically, it should have reached once the idea of linear warfare was resurrected. The construction of all these defences negated any ideas of us ever attacking an enemy. It seemed that a static and largely defensive campaign was envisaged, that the initiative lay with the enemy. However, though we dug holes in the ground, we did not have to live in them, as did our unfortunate fathers in the previous war.

The senior NCO's in our company evolved a lucrative (for them) early-morning sideline. Ostensibly it was aimed at bringing a little cheer into the impending grey days of the lower ranks. We tried not to laugh when their spokesman, in putting forward the "suggestion", said that they were only concerned about our comfort. We did not dare to accuse them of lying.

The workers in our company were woken up on hoar-frosted, dark mornings for their day's hard work with a mess tin of tea, provided by NCO's to a captive market. Equipped with iron dixies, containing freshly brewed tea, ready change and note pads they invaded the unheated billets of the sleeping herd at six am. A customer, prone on his dusty palliasse, would be prodded awake by a crouching warrant officer. An upheld mess tin received a full ladle of hot tea that had been pre-laced with Carnation evaporated milk. If payment for it had to be deferred – on the slate – until pay day, a name would be noted. When challenged tersely for an opinion of the rich brew by a superior straining to be affable, we would honestly admit that tea had never tasted better. Mind you, we would have said so even if it had been made with local canal water, for the names of dissenters would be mentally noted.

One brittle, frozen night, in defiance of an imposed blanket curfew, I decided to visit my favourite estaminet. I would not be missed by anyone who mattered providing I was back in the billet before the early morning tea servers arrived there.

I had been attracted to this cafe, not only by the steak and chips and the beer, which was untypical of French beers, but also by the owner's daughters, Yvonne and Yvette, particularly the dark and flirtatious Yvonne. We had become very fond of each other and I had great hopes of getting much fonder.

That part of the attraction faded abruptly one night when I saw her with a poilo who had just returned home on leave. Apparently, he was her fiancee. Yvonne had a poor memory and she had forgotten to tell me about him. I gawped at him as he stood behind the bar, disfiguring the cosy scene. He filled the open doorway, almost blocking out the infiltrating light from the greater illuminated kitchen behind him. He was very well made and set up, and not a shapeless lump like so many abnormally big men. Given cause, my suddenly-acquired rival could easily throw me bodily through the window. Reminded that we were supposed to be allies, I hastily transferred my shallow affections to the hovering, blonde and petite, Yvette.

Joyfully anticipating seeing Yvette again over a meal served on a plate instead of one plonked into my big mess tin, and having a drink poured into a glass rather than one swilled into the smaller mess tin, I crept out of the billets. Shod in soft leather slip-on shoes I ran to the cafe.

Much later that night, flushed with warmth, food and beer, the cold air stinging my cheeks, I patted back to my spartan billet. The streets were silent and the pavements glistened with frost in the moonlight. The air was clear and smelled clean. The haunting refrain of Plasir d'Amour, played on a scratched gramophone record during the meal, endlessly repeated itself in my ears. The evocative sadness of the melody complemented my reflective mood. I wondered where I would be next month, next year, the next decade?

The next tenth of a second I was yanked into a slit of an opening between two houses by someone with the strength of a gorilla. My assailant then embraced me. It was the provost sergeant who had recently been attached to the company, and who was about to bring me back to harsh reality.

Squatty and powerfully built, his small, coconut head had been jammed directly onto broad shoulders. He had a massive chest and long thick arms. Deep set eyes, bushy eyebrows and a protruding lower lip cast him as vaguely simian. He would have intrigued Darwin.

The sergeant policeman boxed as a light-heavy. His three stripes merely acknowledged his ability in a square ring for he was generally considered to be not very bright. Nevertheless, Bullet Head had ably caught me.

Crushing my biceps with his hydraulic clamps, he shoved me hard against the cold wall. "I've been waiting for you, Cotton," he said, making a common error in the pronunciation of my surname, "you're breaking curfew again."

"Sorry, Sarg," I managed to blurt out.

"Sergeant," he corrected, "don't short change me, you streak of wind. This is not the first time you've got out. Your mates have been covering for you, haven't they?" There was enough light for me to see that he had screwed his little eyes into tungsten tipped drills.

"No boots, no cap," he continued in a dangerously mild voice, ignoring the glengarry slipped under an epaulet of my battle dress tunic. He started to bellow into my face about the hidden perils of fraternisation, no doubt spitefully since it held none for him. A bedroom window across the street opened, and then slammed shut.

In a sinister change of tone he asked: "Now, do you want me to report your absence from billets and being improperly dressed, or do you want it sorted out in the back yard?" His thumb arced to indicate the open space at the other end of the entry.

That would be his preference. To him, active military policing was a labour of love, whereas writing reports about it afterwards was not.

He released the pressure on my numbed biceps. I was still pressed against the wall of the narrow entry. Neither of us could comfortably turn sideways, he particularly with his east-west development.

To strike a superior officer was a serious offence, but I was unlikely to commit it since I would be giving away two stones. Another disadvantage was my vulnerable left hand, injured in an industrial accident. If it was going to be jabbed against his hard head, it ought to be protected with a glove. Even if it was, I might discover in that secluded back yard that I had "round heels" and that the tooth fairy would be visiting me later.

I hadn't a snowball in – I feintingly lunged to one side, sprang over to the other, leapt out into the street, and ran. Swiftly glancing over my shoulder I saw that he was lumbering unevenly after me. He seemed to have not quite mastered the art of running in an upright position.

I was awakened early next morning by a burning sensation on my face. I 'escaped' from my burning carrier to find a ladle of hot tea being held against my ear. As my room mates gently snored I was issued a warning by the kneeling provost sergeant who, on his attachment, must have bruised his way into the tea racket.

He regarded me with a smile of gratified malice as he hissed his message, the words sliding out on their backs: "If I should catch you out after curfew again, I shall say I found you lying in a pool of blood at the foot of some stone steps."

With that promise he half-filled my upheld wavering mess tin, leaned back on his heels and said openly and sweetly, and with a look of pure hate spreading menacingly across his unlovely features, "Pay at the end of the week, Cotton?" (As in reel.)

CHAPTER 6

The territorials sent hurriedly to France to join the BEF had had scanty training and were short of equipment. To bolster them, one battalion was lifted out of a territorial brigade and replaced with a regular unit. In February 1940, the 2nd. Battalion, Royal Warwickshire Regiment, was transferred to the 144 Brigade, 48th. Division. The battalion was brigaded with the 5th. Gloucestershire and 8th. Worcester Territorials. We naturally had hoped to have formed a complete brigade of a regiment with our 7th. and 8th. Territorial Battalions but that, it was perhaps seen, might localise battle casualties instead of spreading them.

The transfer effected, we moved to our new billets at Leforest, a mining village on the northern outskirts of Douai. It was a march of twenty miles in bitterly cold weather for our footslogging comrades.

In March it became the battalion's turn of duty in the Saar sector. To conserve the tracks of our carriers, we travelled en bloc to Metz by train with our vehicles in tow on flatbeds. Carrier Platoon personnel were imprisoned for two days and two nights in an uncomfortable, closed truck. When we were under pressure we slid open the door, and hoped that nobody in the truck chattering along in front was doing the same against the wind. As in the Great War, the trucks that transported us were labelled: 'HOMMES 36-40 CHEVAUX 8'. They were probably the same trucks.

The battalion was billeted overnight in a vacated French infantry barracks. The grim, massive square building squatted on a vast parade ground that was ringed by a high wall. The barracks were damp and fetid. The concrete floors were uncovered, the walls bare and, like the ceilings, grey and dirty. Mere holes in the floors served as lavatories. The barrack rooms were devoid of furniture except palliasses. We had stumbled upon a foreign way of barracking troops.

British regular soldiers were not enamoured of their conscripted French allies. They were slovenly and did not march in a soldierly manner but strolled, some of them wheeling bicycles and all of them feeling free to smoke their strong cigarettes and to converse with each other. They were poorly paid and, if Metz was typical of their barracks, badly quartered, which may explain why French troops appeared downcast and resentful when seen straggling along the roads. French Colonial troops we won't even talk about.

We moved up into the Saar region, between the Maginot Line and the Siegfried Line. In this stretch of 'no mans land' the battalion took over an abandoned village to relieve a British infantry battalion, the 5th. Northamptonshire. Front enemy positions were less than 1500 metres from our foremost posts.

The villagers in the forward zone, ligne de contact, had all long since left, some to Germany, others to France according to their lights. The area had a history of dispute and the inhabitants had a flexibility of allegiance.

The eerily silent village had suffered from neglect and looting. Its houses, stripped of everything of value that was easily transportable, had become hovels. There was no livestock and even the birds failed to sing. It was unnatural; as if the village was sulking over the loss of its inhabitants.

The empty houses were again crammed with relieving troops and the remaining bits of furniture in them once again re-arranged to suit particular requirements. The homes of the fled people were treated unfeelingly because they were unlikely to survive undamaged as both sides strove to retain or regain villages between the Lines. The Maginot and Siegfried Lines, incidentally, were not obvious fortified lines, nor were they continuous but, in both cases, were a series of defensive zones with subterranean interconnections. I did not see anything to indicate the French one, and hoped to remain unaware of the other.

We spent a month in the region, alternating turns in the forward zone with those in the support zone, ligne de soutien. It was a surreptitious type of warfare in the forward position, mainly carried out at night, silently probing and scouting on foot patrols. Our carriers were unsuitable for these stealthy operations. Occasionally, and always suddenly, the rural quietude would be shattered by the stutter of machine guns when opposing patrols clashed in the darkness.

Our old platoon commander, Lieutenant, now Captain, Allen, seemed to be permanently engaged on night patrols. He had been transferred to 'D' Company on his promotion. Until he was replaced, 'H' remained in sole charge of Carrier Platoon.

Shelling was light, spasmodic, searching and often inaccurate. It never developed to herald a direct attack on the village during our occupation of it. But we grew to fear the unheard crack of a sniper's rifle. When it was heard, he'd missed.

We, in our billet, brought down all the old beds from the upstairs rooms and butted them against each other in the downstairs rooms. We slept fully dressed with our boot laces slackened. To leave a room at night, for whatever reason, we most of us had to climb over prone bodies to reach an open doorway. The doors themselves had either been removed or flattened to a wall.

At night, every night, those among us who had not blackened their faces to go out on patrol, did their two-hours-on-and-four-hours-off guard duty. Guard duties were carried out indoors, discreetly, and not outdoors where unwelcome visitors might have expected them to be. It entailed sitting on a bed near a strategic window cradling a rifle. The unreal silences on those moonlit nights were deafening. Whispered conversations among us were permitted and talking was not. Snorers were at risk of getting smothered.

Around our detached house we suspended a line of empty tin

cans, in each one of them a pebble, to act as a crude alarm system. German patrols were often accompanied by Alsation dogs, which were far more likely to activate the alarm than their handlers. Fortunately, as our CO dryly observed in Company Orders, an inquisitive German Army dog was itself incapable of reporting our whereabouts.

The raids between our troops and those of the enemy increased in intensity, with no real gains for either side. The furtive warfare was unlike that to be waged uninhibitedly across Belgium, which we found less harrowing – as we advanced, that is. On the retreat to Dunkirk, however, we began to wish that a quest for adventure when enlisting had not been quite so compelling.

One quiet, grey afternoon, when making a routine maintenance check on the entrails of my carrier, I was surprised and triggered to attention by an officer of another company of the battalion. I had cleaned, re-assembled and set the gaps of eight spark plugs and had just refitted the last one of them when he found me. Though shy and awkward in the presence of senior officers, I was flattered to have been sought out by Captain Fisher. Quick of the mark, he had just been awarded a Military Cross for his bravery when leading a night patrol that came upon a German outpost.

Put at 'ease' I listened respectfully to the Captain, curious to know what had brought us together. Standing in the well of my carrier I looked down at the startlingly white, violet, white little ribbon, signifying the recent decoration, that adorned his chest. The small rectangles of two contrasting colours fascinated me.

"I've good news for you, Cottam," he said.

He knew my name, had pronunciated it correctly, and he was smiling. I should have recognised the sign and remembered that dentists always smile when issuing the worst. In any case, it depends from which angle it is viewed whether news is good, indifferent or plainly bad.

"Yes, indeed," he said, beaming at me. "The Old Man has had a brain-wave. He intends using your carrier as an armoured conveyance when he wants to look around out there. I shall probably come along too."

'There', as indicated by his airily waved cane, was a large segment of silent, sinisterly brooding landscape, deserted of cattle and studded with a few copses that merged finally with thin, then dense, uninviting woods inhabited by roe deer and who knows what else. A mist, its grey tendrils spreading, rolled down from these thick pinewoods that covered a slight rise. France, incidentally, was in the opposite direction to where his cane had pointed.

Pleased that I seemed to be taking his notion of good news in the right spirit he prattled on: "Your emasculated carrier is a misfit, you know, not even having a mounting for a Bren, so we are glad that we can find a useful purpose for it."

Emasculated! Misfit! I swear the carrier shook with me at the hurtful descriptions. I had become attached to my meek vehicle and resented it being humbled. Steadying myself I continued to listen fearfully to my harbinger of "good" news, already convinced that the Colonel's brain-wave bore little relationship to common sense.

"A soft-skinned vehicle," said Captain Fisher with another careless and wider sweep of his wand in the wrong direction, "wouldn't get very far out there, would it?" His voice had risen to its mirthful level. A "soft-skinned" vehicle, the rejected alternative, was a fifteen hundredweight truck shod with bullet-proof, solid tyres.

In the full glare of his terrifying smile I closed my eyes and saw things vividly. A Bren-gun carrier, with its wick turned up, did not motor as quietly as a fifteen hundredweight, and that vehicle was no Rolls Royce. If a carrier was essential for this scouting operation, I felt that an armed one would be more suitable. Better still, all nine of them since the enemy would be instantly alerted and a private little battle would ensue.

Armies of old advanced in pomp – colours unfurled, drums beating – to do battle with the enemy. I wondered if our drummers had brought along their ceremonial gear!

Still smiling, Captain Fisher left me. He remained blissfully unaware of my shortcomings, chief of them being an inability to share his wild enthusiasm for tasks smacking of extreme danger. His visit had raised hopes that the covetable job of CO's driver (staff car) was to be offered to me. It was rumoured that the driver of the Humber Super Snipe had been sacked for committing the military crime of contracting VD. That job had now an added appeal since the staff car was classed as very soft-skinned.

For those who like their stories neatly rounded off, I was never once ordered to provide the CO with a reluctant armoured conveyance during that spell in the Saar and Moselle region. For that I was truly thankful.. A reconnaissance party in a noisy carrier in the middle of the day might have just time to pin point the exact location of, say, an anti-tank gun, but would stand little chance of bringing back that information to our lines.

("Pity about that unarmed carrier." "Stout fellows. Couldn't have felt a thing. Another pink gin?")

I would have only one thing in common with the two brave officers, who were my superiors in every respect. Lieutenant-Colonel P.D.V. Dunn, DSO, MC, Captain M.E. Fisher, MC and Private F.T. Cottam were all going to be stretchered out of Belgium.

When the turn of duty was completed, the battalion returned to new billets at Leforest. Carrier Platoon was billeted in an empty barn of a run down farm. We knocked up improvised beds to avoid sleeping on the dank earth floor.

Our carriers, parked in the open in odd corners of the farm, were covered with their tarpaulins. Small branches, cut from brush-wood with our machetes, were strewn over the coverings to soften the outlines of the concealed armour when seen from the air.

A young Pole, who had recently arrived in the district, was hired by the farmer to slaughter the remaining emaciated cattle. We rounded up the cows for the executioner, penned them and led the unutterably sad, mournful beasts, singly every half an hour, into the arena inside a barn.

A cow had its head held downwards by a rope attached to an anchor ring sunk in the concrete floor. The cow was then clouted on the head with a sledge hammer, two or three times depending on a varying resistance to this form of attack. On crumpling, its throat was cut and sad reproachful looks in big brown, gentle and hitherto trusting eyes faded. I had never before seen a cow killed. Never saw one since, either.

Expertly and speedily skinned, the carcass was then decapitated, gutted and hoisted up on a block and tackle to be cleaved in half down the back-bone. The opposite sides were hung on galvanised meat hooks.

It had taken Stefan twenty-five minutes to transform a cow into beef. After offal, pelt, head and hooves had been set aside and blood swilled down a drain, a shout would resound in the barn: "Next!"

The slaughterous Pole was fluent in English and French and he had understood when ordered about in German. Yet in spite of his internationalism, his slightly flattened round face made him appear unmistakenly Polish. His dexterity with a knife made me curious about his exploits on a journey from Poland. Stefan would be a formidable adversary in the dark.

In April the platoon began to trickle home on ten days' leave. Every man in my small party, made up from every company in the battalion, went on leave in full pack and with greatcoat, rifle and bayonet. This was in case of a sudden recall and then perhaps an expedient switch to a different unit.

On this, my only leave from France, Ruth and I were engaged. It was expected of us. We celebrated with a few bottles of Australian white wine and Mam attempted the 'Wedding March' on the organ. "I'll get it right for the day," she promised.

Ruth was a lovely, warm hearted girl. Thrown closer together by our match-making parents, however, we never had time to get to really know each other. Affections between Ruth and me seemed to shrink with distance on my return to France.

Tony, my eldest brother, had joined the RAF and was being trained as an aircraft fitter. During my leave, I visited him at his station, Cardington Camp in Bedfordshire. Directed to his featureless hut, I waited impatiently for him to come off a parade. Being in khaki, I got several curious glances from the blue-uniformed men as they filed in. Tony spotted me and we moved to his corner bed for a little privacy.

"You always said you would prefer the RAF. Did you volunteer to avoid being conscripted into the Army?"

"Yes. But no offence, Owkid. Bill feels the same – he's aiming to be a pilot or navigator."

I had to ask him. "Mam wants to know if you have had –" The reminder brought an anxious half smile to his pale face for a brief moment.

"No, touch wood. I think I am finally cured of it," he said quietly. That was good to hear. Tony had a history of bed wetting that had continued well into his teens. He had to withstand a more miserable life in orphanages than his brothers because of his affliction. The standard institutional remedy for it was a belting, with a leather belt. Perversely, a silent barrack room condemnation would have shattered my sensitive eldest brother.

I stayed with him long enough to feel that he had adapted well to service life, though there was something still set apart about him.

I dozed off on the train coming back and woke up in Derby, so it transpired: all railway station names had been removed at the beginning of the war. I belatedly reported back to Mam that her first-born son was settling down in the RAF and that she had no cause to worry about him.

When my leave ended (it had flown by), Mam, Bill and Dai came along to see me off at New Street Station. A raw wind began to thicken with rain as we walked, late at night, through darkened streets. Bill carried my rifle, which he had slung over a shoulder. On his small frame it looked, in the gloom, like the un-trunnioned barrel of a cannon.

The unwelcoming station was lit with sparse overhead lights that were so dim people's movements appeared ghostly. Locating my train I boarded a carriage and lowered a window. Sticking my head out of it I held my hand melodramatically to brow and said to Mam and my two brothers: "Please, don't look back – I couldn't bear it!"

The train began sighing in its eagerness to separate us. They waved to a sad clown when an unseen guard blew a single note on his whistle and the train lurched forward into smooth motion.

The express train took just two hours to reach Kings Cross Station. The journey to Dover and the eventual sea crossing to Boulogne was comparatively slow.

The last stage of the journey was a very slow, square-wheeled train ride. In the unfamiliar company of men from other units of the BEF, who also had been on leave, I became depressed and increasingly apprehensive about the future, feeling that things were going to erupt when we arrived back. My travelling companions might have been thinking the same for we were an unhappy lot.

We rumbled to a halt at a dilapidated station. Tins of bully beef and packets of hard biscuits were literally thrown into the carriage through an opened window. None in the compartment had a tin opener. I debated whether to eat my emergency rations, concentrated chocolate in a flat tin. Following the example of a resourceful one among us, I attacked the tin of corned beef with my bayonet, gouging out sufficient of the meat to sustain me through a long, dreary, wet night.

Back at the farm, after a gruelling journey, I was greeted by Pugh. He had skidded to a stop, spun his carrier into a 180 degree turn in its own length, and was reversing it into a shaded corner formed by two barns.

"We've just got our new platoon officer, Cush!" he shouted above the whine of the high-revving engine. He's dying to meet you!" Pug's grin conveyed a slight caution. I helped him to cover his carrier with the tarpaulin and then to spread withering foliage over the top of it.

"The new bloke is an ex-racing driver. He has a gammy leg – from an accident at Brooklands He's not a regular, but seems all right."

"At ease. So, you're Cottam - the platoon jester." It was said not so much in acknowledgement, but rather as a warning. He gave me a once over to confirm his prejudgment.

"You are on meals' fatigues tomorrow," he said, without

71

preamble, "bring them from company cookhouse. After the last meal, scour the dixies and pans. I want to see them clean and shining. There are no cleaning materials so scrape some ash from the yard and mix it into a paste. Use plenty of water." In a clipped and upper-class accent he consigned my leave to a distant memory.

Slimly built, 2/Lieutenant D. Lee was about thirty years old. This was his first command and he seemed eager to establish an immediate authority over it - starting with me. (I had to scour those bloody dixies three times before he would pass them as clean.) He reached for his heavy walking stick and leaned on it to raise himself from his seat in the farm kitchen. It was not unusual for officers to carry these regulation-type walking sticks in the field. He was not merely bowing to military fashion, though. He needed that prop. Shortly after I was wounded in Belgium, he became one of the many casualties of the renewed attack.

Lieutenant Allen, his predecessor, was a calm, restrained career officer. He spoke softly and he rarely wasted words. A fair-minded disciplinarian he had attracted the respect, and affection, of all those serving under him. When he left us on his promotion to captain, he took with him his batman, Gunner, nee Drummer, Wilson.

I met Tug, unexpectedly, in a Birmingham department store just after the war had ended. Through that campaign in Belgium he also had lost body weight, one off above the knee. On being fitted with an artificial replacement limb he had found a job as a lift attendant at the huge store. Later, when it was realised that he had not kept his brains in his missing foot, he was put in overall charge of all the lifts in the building.

We yo-yoed up and down in his lift while reminiscing about our brief war. He told me that Pug's elder brother, a called up reservist in 'C' Company, had also lost a leg above the knee. Pug, himself, having arrived back in one piece, had been sent overseas with a reformed unit to push his luck further still.

Tug said he thought he had seen Captain Allen firing a Bren gun until silenced by a German tank that ran over him, but he could not be sure about this. A wounded Tug had become confused. Officially, he said, his officer, our old platoon commander, was 'missing presumed killed.'

Records now show, however, that on 28 May 1940 Captain Allen was taken prisoner with about 90 soldiers, including over 50 from our battalion. During the retreat they all had been involved in a rearguard action, the Battle of Wormhoudt in northern France. Ordered to "Hold your positions at all costs, to the last man and the last round," to allow others to escape to Dunkirk, they were captured when their ammunition ran out.

The unarmed prisoners were double-marched at bayonet point by a detachment of the infamous SS Regiment, 'Leibstandarte Adolf Hitler,' to a barn on the outskirts of the town. Wounded and unwounded alike were herded into the wooden building and almost all of them were then brutally murdered.

Captain Allen, the only officer among them, was shot and killed after he had dragged the wounded Private Evans, also of 'D' Company, out of the barn. Bert had had an arm shattered when stick grenades had been thrown into the barn. When the officer was shot Bert was also shot, in the neck by a bullet that had been deflected off a tree. In making his escape, he was again shot, this time in his shoulder. Seriously wounded he was later recaptured by less brutal enemy soldiers. Bert's arm was amputated at a hospital in Boulogne before he was sent to a PoW camp in Poland.

I first met Bert when we were stationed in Aldershot before the war. We both were then in 'D' Company. Bert did not go to France with the battalion because he, along with other young soldiers, were under age for active military service. Immediately he attained the age of nineteen he was sent out to rejoin his company. His baptism was that holding operation at Wormhoudt.

Bert was one of the very few survivors of that barbaric deed. Now living quietly in Redditch he still cannot erase the memories of it. And he will never forget the heroism of Captain J.F. Lynn-Allen.

CHAPTER 7

When Germany simultaneously invaded Holland, Belgium and Luxembourg on 10 May 1940, Allied troops responded by moving northwards into Belgium. Active hostilities were about to begin. Generally, there was a sense of relief in the battalion that the 'phoney war' period was at last over.

After frantic preparations had been completed during annoying air raids, the battalion was ordered not to join the initial advance into the old arena of Europe. We followed, in a wave of supporting troops, at dawn on the 14th.

Sensibly, my unarmed carrier was ruled as unsuitable for the real thing and was left behind. Owing to the combined transfer of Captain Allen and Tug Wilson there was a vacancy for a front gunner in Poulton's carrier. I filled it and doubled as a relief driver. Poulton and I were old MT Platoon mates and he was pleased that I joined him. Having two experienced drivers would be comforting should anything happen to one of them.

Though all the drummers had been taught the basics of carrier driving their ceremonial duties had ruled out prolonged training with Carrier Platoon. Driving a carrier at high speed over rough terrain would have demanded of them a greater skill than that required to motor sedately along the Egham bypass.

As dawn dissolved into day the platoon of nine carriers and twenty-seven men was slotted into a long column of brigade vehicles, most of them canvas-covered trucks carrying equipment. The sun rose on our right, and the shadows cast by the vehicles ran beside them, flicking over the hedgerows. Red-capped military policemen, stationed at busy, important road junctions, were directing the traffic on noting the division transfers on vehicles. It was just as if we were going on manoeuvres. The live ammunition for the Bren, three service rifles and the anti-tank rifle, and the primed 'pine-apples' in their various nesting boxes reminded us that we were not going out to play games this time.

Sat next to Poulton in the front cab, I lowered my seat: both front seats could be individually lowered to leave two tin helmets just below the top of the armour-plated surround. My vision was now restricted to a tiny rectangular view through a narrow slit covered with armoured glass. Sighting the Bren gun, I aimed at dummy targets, in preparation for having to fire at real ones, instantly.

We clattered along slowly in the convoy, just about able to motor in top gear without labouring the engine. The platoon officer was in the leading carrier followed by 'H' in his. They also were riding 'shotgun'. At noon the shadows cast by the carriers grew lean and moved under their tracks.

We had crossed the frontier, without being aware of doing so, and were now in pastoral country. Farms and small-holdings, hamlets and villages were closely entwined. Windmills and church steeples marked the horizon. Buildings began to sprout along the road, becoming more numerous as they channelled us into Tournai.

After we had passed through Tournai I noticed that hot water was seeping out of the radiator, which was at the back of the front cab. I nudged Poulton. "The radiator's sprung a leak," I said.

He glanced down at the pool of rusty-looking water forming on the deck. "Better to have problems like this now rather than later," he said quietly without a change in his expression. He was a true stoic.

The engine was smelling hot as we dropped out of the convoy and scrounged some water for the radiator from anxiously helpful people lining the roads. They treated us like heroes, but it was unearned gratitude, and was doomed to remain so.

We now had to crawl to wherever we were supposed to be going to avoid overheating the engine. Although the road junctions were now denuded of assertive redcaps, and though our carriers were not linked by radio, we never felt lost in this strange country. Destiny, it seemed, was leading us.

The lone military vehicle passed through Am, Enghien, Hal and reached the outskirts of Brussels. We parked in a street of shops. Leaving our mate in the rear seat, Poulton and I went in search of food and drink now that we had to fend for ourselves.

Again, the people were overwhelmingly kind and generous to us. Laden with fresh baguettes, butter, cheese and a bottle we hurried back to our carrier for it had attracted a horde of curious, elated children. Before we were able to lend a hand to repel juvenile boarders we were baulked by a small crowd of people that had gathered near our parked carrier.

In the centre of this agitated assembly was a protesting man wearing British Army battledress. The enclosing people were jabbering excitedly. When they spotted Poulton and me they tugged us toward the central figure, the man dressed like us. He had the look of a trapped animal. He was small, young and was red-faced with embarrassment, or fear.

We could follow neither the many rapid conversations in the Flemish tongue nor a particular one at a patient, dictation speed, but their drift was ominously unmistakable. The captive was being accused of being either a fifth columnist or a German spy. The people wanted us to interrogate him in English to establish if he was, as apparently he maintained, genuinely a British soldier.

We first asked him his name. He stared back at us uncomprehendingly, his face reddening to a deeper hue. In a further attempt to test his authenticity we rattled off: rank, number, unit? Our voices roughly synchronised the standard question. Again there was no response and he turned to his captors and resumed arguing with them in Flemish, the only language he spoke. He definitely had spoken, through inability or choice, no English and, apparently, no French or German either.

A small, thin man with penetrating eyes above an aquiline nose said to me, in simple French, that the captive had offered no satisfactory explanation why he was wearing a British uniform. Grabbing my arm, and with his keen eyes darting birdlike, he pointed out the absence of shoulder flashes or other insignia denoting a unit or division on the man's brand-new khaki battledress, and that his brand-new ammunition boots were dull and dimpled. But was this enough to prove the man's guilt?

It was, however, extremely unlikely that the British Army had a foreign unit in its midst whose members would refuse, when asked by allies, to identify themselves or offer proof of identification. The Belgians were justifiably worried about the emergence of fifth columnists in their country and this man could not – dare not? – explain why he was wearing a British Army uniform.

The crowd had grown larger. Some of the men, feasibly of the militia, had reaquainted themselves with service revolvers. These weapons looked strangely out of place, ungainly and ugly in civilian hands. They dragged the summarily convicted impostor away. Poulton and I exchanged anxious glances. I had the uneasy feeling that the prisoner, whoever or whatever he was, had just moments left to live.

"What do you think his chances are?" I asked Poulton.

He shrugged his shoulders in acceptance. "About nil, I should think."

We drove on and skirted Brussels. The carrier rocked gently as we rattled over the paves. We found a big forward base of the BEF in the open countryside. A great number of men with their equipment were assembling here before passing through. We found a Service Corps temporary workshop and got the leaking radiator of the carrier patched up. We were told where to look for our unit.

Just as we were about to move out of the busy base, German dive-bombers came screaming out of the afternoon sun. Everyone ran to take cover. I chose an adjacent field in which to flatten myself, reasoning that vehicles and fabricated buildings would be the main targets for the enemy planes.

Raising my head a little I could see the bombs dropping in forward curving flights from the crooked winged Stukas and the wheel-spatted JU87's. I was ready to move swiftly to avoid the missiles that shuddered the ground on exploding. The contrived screaming of the diving ugly black Stukas was terrifying as they bombed at low level, pulling out and up into a tearing climb. It was said that the pilots had had their eardrums pierced to lessen the pain caused by these manoeuvres.

A big shard of hot, burning steel thudded down just missing my head. It was recognisable as a piece of a heavy anti-aircraft shell casing. If it had landed on my head, this narrative might not have been written.

The anti-aircraft gunners in the next field were blazing away. I saw one plane hit and blown to pieces, and then heard distant cheering. Another dive-bomber limped away, smoke trailing from it. Then, one of the light gun emplacements, a Bofors, received a direct hit. The poor gunners really were thrown up in the air like discarded rag dolls.

There was no retaliation from our own, stretched Air Force. Only once during the campaign in Belgium did I see our fighter planes engage in dog fights, and that was a fiercely contested aerial battle above Ohain Wood. "Where are our own fighter planes?" the familiar cry would be repeated until it became obvious to all, the sky belonged to the hostile planes of the Luftwaffe.

Late that night we rejoined our platoon and the battalion at Waterbosch.

"You managed to get here then," said 'H' gruffly, withholding a smile to disguise his relief.

During the following night the battalion moved, through Waterloo, to La Hulpe. In the afternoon we took up positions at Foret de Soignies. Everyone in the battalion was tired. We had had little sleep and almost no food in the previous thirty-six hours. Those marching in columns suffered the most. It was a broiling hot day.

The next few days were condensed to a kaleidoscope of intense experiences as we were thrust further south. We took up positions only to be withdrawn hastily to take up new ones. Driving through the day became frustrating, The roads were choked with trudging refugees who restricted the passage of columns of military traffic.

The absence of traffic control points added to the chaotic road conditions. On a narrow road, a French, horse-drawn, squadron of artillery, teamsters yelling, wheels creaking, overtook us and scattered a column of refugees when the leading whipped horses ploughed straight through them.

The threat of being dive-bombed, then strafed, during daylight hours was with us constantly. The German heavy bomber formations of large two-engine Dorniers ignored us initially as majestically they headed for preselected strategic targets.

Still on the defensive, we now drove mainly at night to new positions from which attempts would be made to hold up clanking, wheezing enemy tanks. We rattled along slowly in pitch blackness, without lights, peering at the newly white-painted differential housing of the vehicle in front. Sometimes we found that the 'diff' of a leading truck would be lit up faintly by a rigged-up tail lamp. This was a welcome navigation aid to a tired-eyed follower.

Very fortunately, Poulton and I were able to share the onus of driving the carrier in these trying conditions. We took it in turns to doze off. Explosions that turned night into instant day for a split second jerked the sleeper awake into a darkness that was a tangible thing.

Somehow, the company cooks managed to provide us with a rare, unexpected meal although they had been the first to suffer casualties. Their main 30 hundredweight truck had been dive-bombed and set on fire. The body of the driver, a French speaking lad from Guernsey, was charred and shrivelled to a third of its living size when eventually extracted from his burning truck.

Through this loss, and other factors, rations had become meagre and then we were reduced to 'living off the country'. We did, just once, have a ration of treacly rum doled into our mess tins from out of a smoking stone jar. To reduce bulk the rum had been concentrated and before using should have been mixed with three parts water to one part of rum to bring it to normal strength. We eagerly drank it neat and then wanted our water bottles filled with the scorching, uplifting spirit. We got no more.

In one organised quest for food, at a deserted village, Lieutenant Lee tried unsuccessfully to blow the lock on the front door of an abandoned shop with his .38 Smith & Wesson revolver.

"It's often done in films," he said with a waning confidence.

'H' rolled his eyes heavenwards despairingly and with a burst from the Bren handed to him he trepanned the whole lock out of the door.

In mock politeness he said, "After you – sir."

Another misleading feature of heroic European war films is the panoramic battle scene displaying thousands of men, hundreds of tanks, transport of all kinds, field guns of various calibres and auxiliary equipment. A posed general, grizzled and red-tabbed, is usually shown viewing his entire, dispersed command from a remote position. Great cinema, but not authentic.

We in Carrier Platoon found that our views were restricted to a street length in built-up areas and to a few fields in the countryside. There was always something, buildings, woods, hills, blocking the view. Our company was invariably the limit of our military horizon. Often, we seemed to be defending in complete isolation, separated from the rest of the battalion with our fears and dangers undiluted.

Carrier Platoon edged along a Belgian airfield. Fighter planes were arranged in neat rows, ready for take-off. They would never again do so. The ground-based planes had been strafed and some of them were still burning. The gnat-like attentions of the small number of surviving Belgian fighters did not bother the mighty German air armadas.

There were no orderly days and nights. Chaos reigned in bright sunshine and it was merely subdued in blanketing darkness.

We paused at Goyck and then stopped briefly at Herrines. Contact with the rest of HQ Company was sometimes regained as we retreated.

The roads were now almost impassable, clogged with worn-out refugees. Clinging to the main arteries under a blazing hostile sun they were a pitiful sight: the old, the young, children. Homeless, crushed in spirit, tired and footsore they were being pushed along by a threatening, advancing enemy. As far as we were ever able to see, the long columns on the congested roads had no ends and no beginnings. Old, dilapidated cars, overladen with extraordinary jumbles of household goods, groaned along in low gear. Bikes, impossible to ride, were loaded with dangling personal possessions. Wheelbarrows and rescued old prams were piled high with hastily selected valuables from abandoned homes. Most in these sad processions were dressed in layers of unnecessary clothing for hot weather: it was the only way to carry additional salvaged clothes.

Straggling, dejected Belgian soldiers were woven into the disorderly long columns. Tagging along, apparently, were fifth columnists equipped with portable radios to monitor the movements of Allied troops.

Where were the refugees going in this fierce summer heat? We, ourselves, would at least be aware of our next destination, even if it was likely to be a brief halt. The poor, confused people could have no set plans. There was nowhere for them to go. They were simply on the move to get away from the always proximate front line, if there was such a thing as a 'line'. Agonised humanity drifting like frightened cattle to avoid getting trampled on. Hastily dug roadside graves were the final resting places of some of them. The haggard, empty, blank faces of the aged, the hunted expressions of those younger, and the appealing bewilderment of the children, when awake and not being carried while asleep by their parents, created a canvas of unimaginable misery, and hopelessness.

Engines revving, clutches slipping, our platoon had to force its way through the people congesting the roads to leapfrog to our next defensive positions. The Belgian's joyful acceptance of the relieving Allied troops that had entered their country had now turned to derision. A wizened old lady, shrivelled in her grief, with eyes that seemed to flame in her face, leaned over the cab and spat at me contemptuously.

The tumult-confused people would not move to the side of a road to let us pass. Perhaps it was thought we were running away.

The attacking speed and the fluidity of modern warfare, which had impressed us, had confounded and disorientated the ordinary people of Belgium. They responded only when attacked by ferocious dive-bombers that stormed out of a dazzling sun and machine-gunned them after dropping their bombs. At their approach, a swirling river of panic-stricken refugees instantly divided lengthways, as if cleaved down the middle, in its mad scramble to forsake a main road and seek comparative safety in the ditches or fields. Not all were quick enough to escape death or injury from these attacks and there were no available medical services to alleviate their sufferings.

Given a split second warning of an attack, we in our carriers also vacated a road, when able, feverishly cutting across cornfields and pastures. Often we dispersed cows that no longer contentedly chewed but herded instinctively. With their heads pointing in the same direction, they would be lowing to be milked. MT drivers were not always able to follow us. Trucks had neither the minimum turning circle nor the ability of a tracked vehicle to cross ditches, to claw up steep embankments.

The shortage of food, and the lack of sleep, and being harried, shelled, bombed and strafed had fuelled a suspicion that the tide of war had turned against us. We did not know, being ordinary soldiers in the field, that the Germans had also attacked through the 'impassable' wooded defiles of the Ardennes, and, having poured through the defensive gap, were now beginning to encircle, squeeze and push us towards the coast and possible annihilation. It could be argued that the Allies had been lured into neutral Belgium when the unfolding German strategy was revealed to our leaders as an inverted variation of the classic Schiefflen Plan that was used in 1914.

The lengthy periods without sleep and being under the stress of fearful excitement insidiously lowered an ability to remain awake during the quieter moments of dark nights when we were not actively engaged in repulsing the enemy. On stag one night, I lay face down up a bank of a roadside ditch. Holding my head up, I strained to detect sounds or movements along the road. Lulled by a soft, warm breeze, I fell asleep. The crumping of distant exploding shells and the unmistakable rat-tat-tatting of nearer machine guns had failed to keep me awake.

'H' woke me up. He had eased his revolver out of its holster and threatened to shoot me with it if I again fell asleep while on guard duty.

"A sleeping sentry could cost the lives of the whole platoon," he said.

He had issued that semi-serious warning on shrewdly sensing that I needed stiffening up. I was the youngest of his drivers and he had always been mindful of my age. For my part, I was grateful that he was at the helm. We were relying on our immediate superiors to steer us safely out of this tempest.

Once again I fell asleep. This time it was with a permission that was suddenly revoked as I slept. We had arrived, just before dawn, at a deserted barn and had settled down to snatch a couple of hours sleep. We had just lain down on our ground sheets, it seemed, when orders came through to move out. As the swiftly assembled platoon was about to move off in the early morning freshness it was noticed that Cush Cottam was missing. Cush was just about to be served a four-course meal by a lusty, busty waitress.

"Cush! Cush!" There was such an urgency in the sergeant's tone that it broke through the haze of my heavenly dream. I quickly gathered my wits and gear as some more home truths were bounced off me.

We reached Papignies having safely got over the bridge leading to it before it was blown up to retard the enemy. The battalion, exhausted through hunger, fatigue and want of sleep, made preparations to stand and fight. It was there just a few hours when it was suddenly withdrawn at midnight. Our trucks had left earlier. Only the carriers and some AA trucks remained in forward positions.

An ack-ack truck was a fifteen hundredweight fitted with a tripod-mounted Bren gun in its loading bay for 'hosing' enemy aircraft with tracers. At dusk it was dismaying to watch yellow-red tracers climbing unhurriedly and failing to reach fast approaching bombers. It was small comfort knowing that only one in five bullets of the thirty in a curved magazine were actually of the tracer type.

The AA trucks withdrew leaving just Carrier Platoon in the forward position. The men, asleep on their feet, were still straggling back burdened with their equipment. They were at peril of being cut off by the enemy. They should have been transported swiftly by the RASC. As was officially recorded, the men were a sorry sight. Their promised RASC troop carriers arrived eventually, and took them over the Dendre to Hollain, a village about four miles south of Calonne.

Meanwhile, the battalion's trucks, which had started out earlier, were dive-bombed when caught in a massive traffic jam on entering Tournai. Vehicles, mixed with refugees, had been packed in four lanes. All 'C' Company trucks were destroyed and the battalion's ammunition was truck blown up. Many of our men were killed or wounded. The 2nd. Gloucesters had a great number of their men trapped in lorries. We would see evidence of the carnage when later we had to pass through the city on our way to rejoin the battalion.

Withdrawn from Papignies, we re-entered a transformed Tournai. Houses were still burning as we thrust our way through the oldest city in Belgium. Some had tumbled into the streets and had mementos of their occupiers scattered in the ruins. Burning, burnt and wrecked vehicles, military and civilian – but mostly military – were half buried in rubble. No sign of life, just the bodies of those who had once lived in hope and then ran in fear as they were deliberately machine-gunned from the air to increase chaos. There were many injured after that attack by the Luftwaffe. Our MO, Captain Crook, caught in the trapped convoy, had attended to many casualties, civilian as well as military.

We were alone in this part of the devastated city. A lull in the shelling had brought a heavy silence, ominous, eerie and scalp-tingling. We had to get out of Tournai somehow. The smoke and the dust made it harder to negotiate the mounds of rubble in the streets. Fortunately we were in carriers not trucks.

Pausing, warily, we searched for food in the least-damaged

houses. We found laden tables for similar meals and saucepans on ovens. Washing fluttering on clothes' lines was another indication that the people had fled in a tremendous hurry, leaving only their Mary-Celeste ghosts.

Looting was simply unthinkable. We transgressed and searched for food only, bread, butter (even if it was slightly off), cheese and fruit for instant consumption and tinned goods for standby. Pilfered coffee would be a welcome additive to boiled water.

Scrambling out of Tournai we crossed the canalised Escaut River to reach Hollain, rejoining our weary, battered battalion mere. The sun was blazing as our depleted platoon entered a lifeless village. Most of its inhabitants had fled a few days previously.

A section of carriers, now presumed lost, had failed to regroup after the rest of the platoon had crossed one bridge that was immediately blown afterwards. Clancy, one of our best drivers, was among the missing men.

An amiable, flamboyant character, he had a studied languid manner. Older than myself, the handsome Clancy had jet-black curly hair swept back from his forehead. The top of his battledress tunic was left unbuttoned to theatrically expose a white silk scarf. On this 'cravat' lay his driving goggles, unlike us pedestrian types whose goggles, when not in use, clasped the domes of our steel helmets. Another thing that marked him out was his disdain for cigarettes. He smoked a short, curved pipe. Losing Clancy was particularly saddening for his fellow drivers.

*   *   *

In the cooling evening breeze we spaced our six remaining carriers along the main road, looking over it towards the almost parallel Escaut Canal. A big gap between buildings on the other side of the road gave us a wide arc of fire across the open ground to the canal, which was less than 200 metres away. Unexpectedly, the canal, which was about 25 metres wide, was of little defensive value against the advancing Germans because the water in it was very low, so that barrier would not prove much of an obstacle to a relentlessly advancing enemy.

The battalion was dispersed so thinly in and around the village that we seldom saw any of our regimental comrades. The few we did see were rounding up skulking fifth column suspects to send back to Brigade HQ for questioning. Passing by with their prisoners, they shot us sparse news of casualties and a warning of an added danger. Enemy soldiers disguised as refugees were said to be infiltrating our lines. That was the only live contact we had with the rest of the battalion. As we were not wired to HQ Company, official communication was maintained by runners. Soon, this would be the only means of contact for all platoons and companies of the battalion when field telephone wires were cut by shellfire too frequently to be repaired.

Constant withdrawals had lowered raised spirits. We were hungry, dirty and dog-tired. Yet, there was a feeling of intense, nervous exhilaration when we were ordered to stand-to. A mass of menacing tanks had been reported to be crawling towards the village. We made our preparations for the impending battle knowing that our position had to be defended whatever the cost. There were to be no more phased withdrawals.

With a wry grin Poulton said: "The only way out of here will be on a stretcher – if we're lucky."

Sadly, he wasn't.

The waiting, the loneliness began to still our voices. We became jittery. Mercifully, we were unaware that the approaching enemy would greatly outnumber the defenders of the village.

I was eating a lump of scavenged cheese as I sat on the neglected front lawn of a detached house that faced the road when 'H' shouted "Catch!" and tossed me a ransacked tin of fruit. "Sorry there's no custard to go with it," he said facetiously. "Tomorrow we'll be back on hard tack."

That was the last time he spoke to me directly.

I used my bayonet tin-opener to get at the fruit. When it was eaten, I plunged my yet-to-be-fixed side-arm into the earth and lay back and laced my fingers behind my head. During those empty, tense moments I began to think morbidly about – bayonets.

A 'fixed' bayonet becomes a terrifying weapon. A bullet can maim or kill impersonally from a great distance. A bayonet has a maximum range of a mere two metres. It is a proximate, a personal weapon. Something about the nameless man attacked with it could scar the memory of the victor. I had used my bayonet only as a kitchen utensil and for chopping wood for outdoor fires. The next confrontation with the enemy's rolling armour, however, could culminate in savage duels with its following slavish foot soldiers, whose bayonets, incidently, were similar in shape to ours, and as long.

The differing infantry bayonets of all armies were long, the length of a dinky Roman sword. The French bayonet was round, having no edge, just a point, a spike rather than a blade. It would be useless for chopping wood. It could inflict a wound that might be self-sealing and then, possibly, self-healing. That was something perhaps overlooked at Bayonne where the bayonet had been evolved from the thrusting of a dagger into the muzzle of a musket. To increase its effectiveness the British bayonet, 1907 pattern, was thoughtfully fluted. The Italians used a sleek, three-cornered weapon. Though it could create an open wound it was, like the French weapon, unsuitable for creating firewood.

In peace-time we had spit and polished our bayonet scabbards with Cherry Blossom to the mirror-like perfection of our ammunition boots. Bayonet blades were burnished until they shone as if chromium plated. It was not necessary to hone them to a razor sharpness since they could be driven through oaken doors when propelled by weighty Lee-Enfield rifles. When training we had charged with fixed bayonets at suspended straw dummies and were encouraged to look fierce and to yell our heads off in order to instill fear into our imaginary foes as we were about to pierce jute sacking.

"Stick 'im! In, twist, out! And the next one! In, twist, out! Too close? Chin 'im with the butt! If you have to use your hands and feet, go for eye balls and low balls. Remember – kill or be killed!" The sergeant instructor, normally an amiable character, had transformed himself amazingly into a ferocious-looking killing machine, divested of all traces of humanity. As he coldly demonstrated, bayonet fighting is a very serious business and one would be looking serious when going about it for only a future tenant of a rubber room would smile as he bayonets someone.

Afterwards, while standing easy, the sergeant said that just the first two inches of steel would be sufficient to disable or kill an opponent. It is not necessary to pin him to a wall. The farther a bayonet goes in, he said, the harder it is to get out. And while you're struggling to extricate your weapon you are leaving yourself vulnerable to an enemy's. Two bloodied inches! That was hardly likely to be accomplished, if indeed it was remembered, when earnestly applying the beautifully balanced, fiendish combination.

To me, the bayonet is the single, important thing that epitomised the sheer horror of the Great War. It stands above the scything machine gun, the spiralled barbed wire, or a deep, waterlogged trench with a scampering bloated rat. The fixed bayonet is a fearful, chilling weapon.

I withdrew mine from the lawn it had ventilated, weighed it, and returned it to the scabbard, uncomfortably aware that my tin-opener cum wood chopper might soon have to be used for its proper, sinister purpose.

The good news was that the three missing carriers turned up early in the evening. The crews had had some hair-raising experiences while tagging along with other units. All of them were glad to be reunited with the platoon, to herd for safety, to share dangers with reliable mates. Their separate experiences gave the rest of us something to talk about, which helped us to take our minds off what we could expect shortly.

The sun was setting against a flaming sky of crimson, purple and pink. Then, twilight faded into dusk. Shelling throughout the night was continuous. Although it was not heavy it made us keep our heads down. Sleep was fitful as shells swished by in both directions. There was an artillery duel in progress, which our side seemed to be losing.

We were again at stand-to in the half light of an early dawn. A haze, prescient of another hot sunny day, hung over the village. Soon, glorious weather enhanced the apple blossom and made the air heavy with its scent. It seemed macabre to fight a battle in this lovely setting. Nevertheless, the Battle of Hollain was about to begin. And many soldiers would end their lives here.

The uneventful and often 'boring' days of pre-war soldiering seemed very far off now. They *were* the best of times.

CHAPTER 8

A notable military historian maintained that Monday, 20 May 1940, was for the democracies probably the most disastrous day of the war. Reference in this case means confirmation for it was definitely the most disastrous day of my brief war.

Though we were still at stand-to as dawn broke we managed to prepare a stew out of our remaining individual rations of hard tack, bully beef and hard biscuits, and with the last of some vegetables we had scrounged on our way south. Everything went in, except sump oil. The larder was now empty and we could not leave our posts to do more foraging.

During that long morning the brew, in a petrol tin dixie, simmered quietly over a wood fire in a neglected front garden of a house that lay back from the road. Early in the afternoon, just as we were quickly devouring our food, the shelling became heavy, and then very heavy. Shells roared overhead and screamed in their plunge to the land, throwing up fountains of earth that hung for moments, and fell apart. A keen observer in the platoon suggested that some of own shells could be falling short and onto the village. Not that it mattered then from which direction a shell came, or if they who sent them wore shallow tin helmets or round coal-scuttles on their heads. When a shell, of whatever denomination, lands, it will very likely go bang.

As the village was being re-modelled we were ordered to take cover. Everyone in the platoon crowded into a cellar of one of the houses at our rear. While that bombardment raged we had no fears of stick grenades being rolled down the cellar steps to greet us and of the survivors getting picked off as they emerged into dazzling sunlight.

Cramped in our temporary shelter we waited for the barrage to lift. But the shelling continued becoming, as was afterwards evident, uncannily accurate. The shrieking incoming shells and the loud explosions achieved crescendo of continuous, ear-splitting noise that almost removed the power of thought. The cellar shuddered and complained and the suspended unlit light bulb danced to the tune of exploding shells.

Insidiously, over the past few demoralising days it had become the man and not the trappings of rank that carried weight with us. In this new democracy I felt free to offer advice to our platoon officer.

"We ought to move out of here, sir," I shouted into his ear, "otherwise we may get buried alive!" It was the first and only time I had shouted at an officer. It had always been the other way round.

He seemed to think hard about the suggestion, and his face was creased by the pressure of responsibility. Another shuddering explosion, the nearest one yet, which amazingly did not bring the building down upon us, helped to concentrate his mind.

"I think you're right, Cottam!" he shouted back. "Everyone move out!"

We filed out of the untenable cellar, stepped over ceiling plaster and rubble and burst out into the dusty, warm air. As we did so, the barrage lifted. The dust began to settle slowly and the sun in a blue sky empty of clouds glared down at us. It was now ominously quiet.

The devastation was something undreamed of except in nightmares. The house we had just left was one of the few with a roof still clinging to it. The building had been extensively damaged and the windows were blown, but by remaining upright it looked oddly out of place. The roads were shell-holed and covered with debris. Telephone wires necklaced from drunken poles.

We saw a lone Westland Lysander 'spotting' aircraft serenely circling above. We had seen this little co-operation plane with

Allied markings the previous day but were unaware that it had been captured and was being used against us to direct mortaring and shelling. During the following turbulent days the malevolent plane was to keep our battalion particularly under surveillance.

Under cover of that last, softening-up barrage the bold and resourceful enemy soldiers had forced a crossing of the canal. Grey-clad figures were seen moving swiftly into attacking positions. They had found those they had been seeking.

We all ran to our stationed carriers intending to board them and to put down a withering defensive field of fire with the mounted Bren guns, those of them that had escaped damage during the shelling. Before we reached our armoured vehicles, however, we were mortar bombed. We were drenched in salvos of small mortars. It was impossible to climb aboard any of the carriers while these diabolical things rained down upon us. To have done so, to then share a steel container with a mortar, would have proved fatal. We lay under the lees of the carriers to wait for the mortaring to let up.

With the now familiar surging of quickened senses, of delight tinged with fear and apprehension, I had swallow dived and landed alongside our carrier, parallel with the nearside track. The slightly raised roadway ran across my view.

These little mortars did not explode loudly on impact. They seemed to snap open: Snap! Snap! Snap!

Unlike a bullet, which has to 'see' a target in its trajectory, a lobbed trench mortar 'looks' for those wishing to remain unseen. I saw the trailing blue-grey smoke of mine, solely mine, as it hurtled down. It was numbered 5110415 and it snapped open to make a small crater in the dry, powdery soil – just to my left.

There was a clang as my left boot, with a sizable chunk of foot still inside it, hit the armour-plated side of the carrier and, simultaneously, there was a heavy, chain-like rattling noise as the track I had sheltered near was severed and whipped off its bogeys and flung contemptuously over the carrier as if it had been a silk ribbon.

As suddenly as it had started to rain hellish trench mortars, it stopped. Dazed, bemused, I sat up – slowly and painfully. The artificial stimulus administered by the short, sharp action had worn off leaving me with a drained feeling. I forced myself to think: I had to assess the extent of my injuries. Most of the blast from the exploding little trench mortar had passed over me to damage the carrier. Even so, I was a bloody mess.

I had lain on my stomach with my head turned to the left. My left cheek was now bloodied having been peppered with fine splinters of shrapnel. I covered my right eye and was relieved to find that I could still see out of the other one. My left elbow had been injured, but it could be bent, if painfully. Exposed left foot ended abruptly like a broken sculpture. Something amiss with my left knee-cap for it was painful to bend that leg. Right foot, still in its boot, numbed and grotesquely loose at the ankle joint. Weirdly, the small explosion had rent my clothing to tatters. White flesh, and red, blazed at me from shredded khaki. Now that I had been brought to a calamitous halt in a forward position of a fluid front line, remote from medical aid, I felt there were long odds against me seeing my twentieth birthday.

A Bren gun began to sing. Alone, on the left side of the left-end carrier in the row, I was then unaware of the extent of the casualties suffered by the rest of the platoon. I realised that there must have been others wounded, perhaps killed, in that short, devastating mortar attack otherwise more Brens would be firing.

I heard the cockney voice of Mat. "Cush! Are you all right!"

I must have made some effort at replying.

In the fellowship of battle, two in the platoon who had escaped serious injury bandaged me with a salvaged field dressing. We each carried one in our battledress uniform. Being young and considering ourselves to be immortal, we had looked upon our field dressings as another useless encumbrance, like our gas masks, to be dragged around. Now that I needed mine, it was useless.

During the lull in the attack I was laid on the back of an open-top fifteen hundredweight truck that had arrived as if in a dream. I was wedged between two other seriously wounded men, one of whom was Killer. He was unbandaged and there were no bloodstains on him. His news was bad. Among the killed was 'H'. Six carriers had been lost through the shelling and mortaring. Effectively, Carrier Platoon had been eliminated by the enemy.

(Long afterwards, when speculating with another survivor of that mortar attack, I maintained that we had not been the victims of bad luck. The attack, I thought, had been precisely timed and very accurately targeted helped, no doubt, by relayed information from that spotter plane. In either event, random or planned, the attack had not been intended to bring us good luck.)

I rolled my head to look at Killer. It was a long time since I had looked at anyone so closely. He was haggard from lack of sleep and his eyes were blood shot. His pale, unshaven face was dirt-etched.

"Where did you cop it?" I asked, concerned and curious because he was not wearing any bandages.

Still staring up at the cloudless sky he told me. As our immensely-liked sergeant had died instantly from concussion he had involuntarily pressed the trigger of his rifle and the .303 nickel-plated bullet up the spout had struck Killer in the back of his head, and lodged there. And he was able to tell me about it!

We were separated at the forward casualty clearing station, which was housed in a big canvas tent. I could see flapping walls as I lay on the operating table. Each leg was injected, cleaned and stitched and then completely bandaged to the groin. Comparatively minor injuries to face and elbow were not dressed. I was left wearing only a shirt and underpants.

The shelling, which had started again, was creeping audibly nearer. This would be at the time when the Germans, though suffering heavy losses, were crossing the Escaut in greater numbers to inflict more casualties on weakened defenders.

"Sorry, old boy," the young doctor said with admirable self-control, "things are warming up outside. We shall have to leave in a hurry." The steadying coolness displayed by some officers in threatening and dangerous situations was impressive. It was something that l admired, and envied.

He snipped the catgut stitching holding in position the blood transfusion tube inserted in my right wrist. There was no time for more blood, and no time even for the holding stitches themselves to be removed.

Dusk had fallen when I began that slow, erratic journey back to England. It was harrowing journey during my waking hours until I lapsed into a delirium. The hospital trains were over-crowded. RAMC personnel worked feverishly on station platforms that were congested with casualties, most of them on stretchers. There was a shortage of medical supplies and, later on, no medical supplies at all.

I was lifted onto a top bunk bed of my first hospital train. In the bunk below me was a soldier who must have been in great pain. He was crying and yelling alternately. The doctor, who seemed to be working without help, injected him regularly during the dim-lit night. Each time he did so, he injected me, although I was not in great pain.

The tired doctor, whose face showed signs of the strain he was working under, injected me for the last time and wrote something on a label. Tagging it to a button-hole on my shirt he said softly, and encouragingly, "You'll pull through."

He then stood in the gangway and turned his head first one way to announce that there was no more morphine and then the other to repeat the message. For a silenced moment all we heard was the regular clacking sounds of the rails sliding under the carriage wheels. The yelling below started again, much louder now and then it tapered off to crying, and finally to whimpering when, I assumed, he was between consciousness and unconsciousness.

Being virtually numb from my thighs downwards I suffered intense pain only when jolted. I had, however, developed an unquenchable thirst for water. Previously, I had always been hungry. Now, feeling strangely light-headed, I longed for thirst-quenching drinks. I was losing blood, but was then unaware of the connection.

I was put on a stretcher, covered with a blanket and placed down on a busy station platform. After a while I started to yell weakly, first for water and then out of fear. I was afraid of being left behind, placed in the motionless, neat row of blanket-draped stretchers I had noticed at the end of the platform.

I had recalled an orally issued official instruction: if a choice has to be made, save the less seriously wounded. Although it made sense when considered logistically and objectively you could be excused for thinking subjectively when it is yourself who has become a poor comparison. Both my leaden, heavily bandaged legs were reddening and a feeling of unutterable loneliness and helplessness began to eat into me.

An RAMC corporal gave me a mess tin of water, propping me up so that I could drink. He assured me that I would not be left behind on the platform for the enemy to collect. The RAMC would take care of me, he promised. You do not need the urinal bottle, he said. The effort made to avoid being pronounced as dying, perhaps dead, had exhausted me. Thereafter I became quiet.

Late one night I found myself on the back of an open truck with other stretcher cases. Then, I was again put on a train. A direct route to France, or to the coast, should not have taken long. I had not heard any destinations mentioned when I was lifted aboard this train, which made me think that routes could not be scheduled. The frightening noises and the turmoil during those dark nights reinforced that impression.

Medical attention was scant. There were no medical supplies so dressings could not be changed. In remaining undisturbed the risk of wounds haemorrhaging would, at least, be reduced.

The hypnotic chattering of the apparently aimlessly travelling train evoked a music hall monologue. Usually, it was recited by a dinner-suited artiste in front of the curtain as scene changing went on behind it. A repetitive snatch of this ditty, about a railway crash, begun to haunt me as I lapsed into delirium:

Clickitty, clackitty, clack...
We came across the stoker,
Clickitty, clackitty...
We thought that he was dead,

Clickitty, clackitty, clack...
For his arms and legs were missing,
Clickitty, clackitty...
And we couldn't find his head.
Clickitty, clackitty...
And we couldn't find...

I no longer croaked for water as these periods of delirium became frequent. I half heard the train squealing to a stop and then was jolted awake with a stab of pain. "Calais," someone mumbled.

I was carried off the train on my stretcher and placed down on the platform.The darkened station seemed to be in the port complex. The port was under siege and was being heavily shelled, the explosions preceded by flashes of brilliant light that blotted out for a brief moment the blinking of stars. Bright illumination followed swiftly by moments of pitch blackness under a starry sky.

There were strange noises, railway carriages squeaking, vehicles turning and reversing in the gloom. Men were shouting as they moved quickly. I heard French voices and, comfortingly, English oaths. Then, I was lifted, carried and placed down again. During the flashes of bright light I saw a ship's side looming above me and, indistinctly, a gangway. There were sounds of intense activity and of heavy movements as I was lifted and carried aboard ship on my trusty stretcher. I was suffering little pain now and was no longer thirsty, but I felt very tired.

I heard a uniformed member of the Merchant Navy on board reply to a question from someone out of my vision in the poor artificial light of the long cabin. No, he had not been given a destination port, he said. In any case, he thought it would now be almost impossible to sail out of Calais. In his opinion, we should board a ship at the only French port on the North Sea, Dunkirk – if the road from Calais to it was still open.

The ship fretted at her moorings. I was now beyond caring what happened to me. Utterly weary, I slipped back into unconsciousness.

CHAPTER 9

That was the Long Of It. Now we come to the Short Of It. 'It', in both cases, meaning me.

Incredible as it may seem, I had not realised that my legs had been amputated. Phantom limb sensations had falsely retained my feet, calves, knees and a much greater length of thighs than I now possessed. Nobody warned me beforehand about the emergency operation, and no post-operation sickness hinted of it having been carried out soon after my admission to Netley Military Hospital.

Unknown to me and without the consent of parent or guardian, which normally is required for someone under twenty one, my unsalvable legs had been swiftly amputated under a spinal anaesthesia. Nobody told me afterwards, and nobody intended telling me afterwards, that I had undergone desperate and drastic surgery. Inevitably, it had perhaps been reasoned, the patient, if he lived, would find out that he had been sawn in half, and would then feel grateful that it had not been done lengthways.

I had been transformed from a vertical five feet ten inches to a horizontal three feet six inches.There was about eight inches left of each leg – roughly, and the pun is intended. The shock of this discovery did not prove too much for me when cautiously I had raised the linen screen that hung over the front of the wire cage, inserted in the bed to support the bedclothes. Sedation and physical weakness, had softened the blow that I was now legless. On first discovering my loss, however, I must surely have wondered: "Where's the rest of me?"

Both stumps were resting on a big square of surgical gauze. A small square piece of the same material covered each end of them. Carefully, I had lifted the corners of the top gauzes to find that the amputations appeared to have been crudely performed. The blunted femurs were protruding from the pink, red-streaked flesh. What once were two perfectly formed legs were now two ham bones. Clinically. I counted my blessings and felt relieved on finding that the family jewels had escaped indiscriminate injury and the drastic surgery.

The hovering ward sister came to my bedside, intuitively aware that the little proscenium screen on the front of the cage was now no longer necessary. Though impassive and brisk she spoke in a kindly tone.

"Your mother has been informed of – your operation. She should be here tomorrow," she said

The sister then explained why the amputations had been left in what seemed to be an unfinished state. As soon as you arrived here you were operated upon, she said, but you were wounded six days previously, according to the label tagged onto your shirt. During that time gangrene had set in. Owing to this infection the amputations had to be done speedily (I caught the word 'guillotine', and wondered if my hearing had been impaired – it had been but I had heard correctly) and left 'open' to ensure that they would drain thoroughly. When healed, both stumps would have to be re-amputated in preparation for the fitting of artificial limbs. "Yes, you will walk again," she said comfortingly, if not authoritatively, in answer to my unspoken question.

"The remaining splinters of shrapnel in your arm should cause you no trouble. The finer ones in your face should work themselves out naturally."

My mother visited me the next day. She brought along Bill and Dai, my younger brothers. War-time restrictions on travel had delayed their arrival. Tony, the eldest of her four sons, had been unable to join them. He was now stationed 'somewhere in England'. Of those in the inner family circle available, only Judy, our mongrel dog was missing. It was a great pity that she could not have been brought along, too. Left in the token care of unfeeling lodgers, the affectionate animal pined and died prematurely during the two week's absence of her remaining loved ones.

Mam calmly accepted my injuries, so it seemed. The emotional barrier separating us didn't give way. She shed no tears, in my presence, anyway. Perhaps they were not far away. I shed some before, and after, Mam and my brothers returned to their jobs in munition factories. I did not weep because I had lost my legs. I wept because I had not. Let me explain.

Phantom limb pain, as opposed to mere limb sensation, is an unfunny phenomenon. The permanent scourge of arm and leg amputees it may be defined as the conscious feeling that a very painful limb is present – the one that isn't. The intense pains are always in the parts that are missing. Though at times my agonies were alleviated by morphine injections, they caused me to lose the will to live. I lost my appetite for food. Mentally, I began to shrink inside myself.

Alerted about my condition, the busy surgeon who had carried out the amputations came to see me. It was the first time I had met him – consciously. He was not only built like a hill farmer, he had the forthright manner of one. Without the slightest help from me, he worked himself into a rage.

"If you don't eat, you will die!" he bellowed at me. "Is that what you want? Eat your meals. As you get stronger the pains will recede. And stop smoking so many of those damn cigarettes!" With that outburst he stormed out of the ward.

I was more afraid of him than of dying. He had been unable to save a number of severely wounded soldiers brought back from France and he intended saving me, it seemed.

A special diet allowed me to indulge an unusual craving for savoury dishes, induced by physical debility. Would I like a glass of beer? In serving my apprenticeship on French beers, I had favoured the darkest of them. I was offered stout as a substitute but was glad when I had had enough of it. Cherry brandy was suggested and was gratefully accepted.

Pencil sketching became my chief form of therapy. Like my

bedridden father before me, I copied photographs, sketching unimaginatively, hardly a craftsman and certainly no artist. Dad had been much better at it.

The attacks of phantom pains did slowly and gradually decrease in frequency and intensity. Renewed severe pains were halved on their return many months later when each stump was separately re-amputated. After the final healing there would normally be only a heightened awareness of the parts that were missing. This 'memory' of absent limbs would be permanently retained.

Unfortunately, the face-distorting pains, in various manifestations, can strike back without warning, particularly as an amputee gets older. I would suffer less than most amputees even though I had a double potential for phantom pains.

Mam spent most of her time at the hospital visiting the various wards. In the next ward, another young soldier evacuated from France had died after having his leg amputated. Mam felt qualified to comfort the grieving parents in their sudden bereavement. Perhaps she consoled them with my case history.

One evacuated soldier in that ward had been blinded. During a bombing raid on Calais he had been scrabbling around in a dazed condition on the floor of a burning warehouse. The building had been set on fire with incendiary bombs. In rubbing his eyes to see more clearly in the smoke and fumes he accidentally introduced into them some oxide composition, a flammable chemical, that had spilled from a bomb. Again, Mam, being kind hearted and emotional outside her brood, was bonded in sorrow with the lad's relatives.

All the other beds in my ward were occupied by French soldiers. They had been evacuated from Dunkirk. Few of them had been seriously wounded. Mam struggled with her weaker, oral French to converse with them and she introduced me to several of their "walking wounded". They shyly complimented me on my crude ability with a *crayon*.

Instructions descended from my surgeon, 'The Butcher,' as he was generically known, that I should be put on traction. My stumps were individually and completely wrapped in surgical adhesive tape.

Cords were tied to the looped ends of the wrappings. The two cords then ran over separated pulleys fixed to the lower horizontal rail at the bottom of the bed. Attached to each cord was a suspended heavy weight that strove to sit on the polished-wood floor. The object was to pull skin and flesh up the exposed ends of the femurs during a pliable healing process and so increase the length of the stumps before re-amputation. As both of them were very short, an increase in lengths of even fractions of an inch would be rewarding if later it was found possible to fit me with artificial limbs.

Being linked to this lashup was not too discomforting. A bolster pillow shoved against my buttocks and tied to the bed side rails acted as a brake and prevented me from being hauled partially through the vertical bars at the end of the bed and coming to a painful stop. As I tended to creep down the bed I had to be uncoupled intermittently from my tensile loads and dragged back up it.

When red hot needles were being stabbed into my phantom feet, the weighted cords restricted the kicking response of my stumps. Restricting the instant and uncontrollable responses is something that I have found beneficial when being "needled", my particular phantoms. Other sufferers may have their "toes" flattened repeatedly on an anvil.

My mother returned home with her two youngest sons. She might have wondered if more would be demanded of her family should the war drag on to the extent of her last remembered one.

A few days after my twentieth birthday I was told abruptly that, in view of the threat of intensive air raids, it had been decided to transfer me to a hospital in a comparatively safer area. That sunny afternoon the weights were unhooked and the surgical tapes ripped swiftly and painfully off my stumps. My stretcher was slid onto a shelf in the back of an ambulance that was growling impatiently. I was sorry to leave Netley Hospital, the hospital with its own anticipatory landing pier at which I had arrived by ship from either Calais or Dunkirk.

The Royal Victoria Military Hospital, Netley, overlooked Southampton Water. The largest hospital in the world, it catered for over 1,000 patients. The Yanks, who occupied it later in the war, drove their jeeps down the long, wide corridors. The hospital began life with Nurse Florence Nightingale taking charge of it on her return from the Crimean War. In the 1960's a fire destroyed part of it, and the bulldozers did the rest.

My next abode was an institution of some sort. Part of it had been pressed into service as a war-emergency military hospital. That part was just one of the big, ground floor wards. The hospital section had no surgical facilities. It functioned mainly as a convalescent home under the supervision of the local doctor. This institution-cum hospital at Ashurst, near Lyndhurst was half-hidden in a sward of the New Forest. Gorse and heather aproned the forest that shielded the buildings.

Most of my fellow patients were fairly new intakes into the services and were being treated for minor disorders. Two or three others had been slightly wounded on active service. By far the most serious case in the ward, I occupied the corner bed next to the senior sister's office.

The hospital was staffed mainly by conscripted Red Cross auxiliary nurses, who were mainly responsible for the friendly, relaxing atmosphere of the place. Some of the nurses that wore the lavender blue uniform and white bib apron with a huge red cross had cars. When able to scrounge sufficient petrol-ration coupons, they would take their patients out for a sunny afternoon run. Regularly I would be carried carefully to a waiting car.

One of the nurses, a qualified SRN, was a titled lady. Although in retirement when the war broke out, she had voluntarily returned to hospital work when her services were needed. We used to visit her stately old home in her stately old banger.

My legs (the euphemism is less jarring) were healing. Surgical dressings, deftly undertaken by Her Ladyship, who must have been stunning and was still remarkably elegant, were simplified to just cleansing and then re-draping with sterilised gauze. Soon they would heal completely. No one suggested that I be re-stretched on a medieval rack arrangement – not at Ashurst, at any rate.

"We think you ought to get out into the fresh air," a ward sister said to me one bright day. "A nurse will take you out in our bathchair," she said proudly.

Apparently one of the staff had discovered an ancient long bathchair in its cobwebby hiding place. Its four big spoked-wheels were shod with slim, solid rubber tyres. The high-sided, plaited wickerwork bathchair was found to be in surprisingly good condition even though Queen Victoria might once have leaned over it on raised toes to enquire about its gallant occupant. Now I was to be taken walkies in the bathchair, which would have accommodated someone twice my length.

Sunk into the stern of the barge-like relic, with a blanket draped over my lower half, not for warmth but to hide from public view what was missing and therefore save me from possible embarrassment, we sailed into the forest. My escort's apron top overhung the raised handle bar and the clean wholesome scent of freshly starched linen fell off her. She smiled at me approvingly.

We spent many sunny afternoons in the forest. The weather was glorious during that long, hot summer of 1940, and the beauty and natural scenic splendour of the secret woodland glades was breath-taking. The only sounds, in this haven of peace with an atmosphere of timelessness, were of rustling leaves and the chorus of song birds. The peace would be disturbed, however, when roaring, low-flying Hurricanes sped to repel German fighters that were playfully popping barrage balloons over Southampton Docks.

Land Army girls, working in the woodlands, were quietly disturbing in their lumpy, dark-green woollen jerseys and bulging jodhpurs. I stared at imprisoning wool and felt that my general health was improving. This indication had not escaped the notice of the sympathetic, young and plain-looking auxiliary nurse who had now become my outdoor constant attendant.

"I read your medical file yesterday, Eric," she confided one afternoon.

She had shown in other little ways that she had grown fond of me, a fondness perhaps stemming from sympathy. Though flattered by her attraction to me I could not share her deeper feelings, much as I tried.

"Oh yes. Find anything interesting?"

We paused for a while and she leant against a tree trunk. Over her folded arms she looked down at me.

"You're getting better," she said. "You should be fit enough for your re-amps by the end of the year. Incidently, why are you called 'Eric' when the name on your file is Frederick?"

"Eric is the tail end of it. Blame my mother. She called Winston, my eldest brother, Tony. David, my youngest brother is Dai. You can guess what she called the next youngest brother, whose proper name is William."

"What did she call him?" she asked playing along with me.

"Harry!" I said, and we both burst out laughing.

The nurse was a sweet-natured offspring of neglectful and moneyed parents, whom, like the lovely old nursing sister, were mentioned in Burkes Peerage. My sensitive companion desperately longed for affection, if not love. I could only offer affection and it would have been heartless of me to have otherwise misled the doe-eyed submissive nurse, particularly as she was the first person to help me to try and regain confidence in myself.

I was still nominally engaged to marry Ruth, but we two were separating gradually as if by mutual consent. Corresponding infrequently, we each found it hard to pan a loving letter. Ruth was in an invidious position. She risked being treated contemptuously by her shallow-thinking neighbours and factory friends if she broke off her engagement to a wounded soldier. I broke off the engagement at my fourth hospital. We had agreed that we were not suitable for one another.

I spent many hours of the sultry days at Ashurst lying on my bed and gazing up at a white ceiling. Reflecting on a vague future I became despondent. Would I be physically dependent upon others for my care and attention? My fears were not groundless. Even if fitted with artificial limbs, total independence would be unattainable due to my high-up amputations. If each leg had been amputated just an inch or so higher, it would have been impracticable to fit me with limbs after the tidying-up re-amps.

There was also the problem about work, which would be necessary to live properly. The war pension of even a severely disabled ex-private soldier was pitifully small and so had a built-in incentive to add to it.

Uncertainty breeds fear. I had few, if any, assets with which to begin a new life. My disability might prohibit a return to factory work. To get, and hold, a job in an office, if I was able to get about, may entail having to enrol at evening classes to obtain relevant qualifications.

This growing feeling of inadequacy began at Ashurst as my general health improved. I started thinking about my prospects when assessing my ward companions. In civilian life the conscripts were, in the main, professional men, surveyors, engineers, local government officers, etc. Though they were better educated, their superiority was never intentionally and arrogantly pointed out to me, except in one biting and unforgettable instance. Other than that I was gently, humourously, made aware of my shortcomings.

Further education of self, therefore, would have priority when learning to live all over again. By acknowledging my supreme ignorance and resolving to uplift myself, I ceased feeling sorrowful. Why play a tragic role with only myself as audience?

A creased photograph of me lying in my long bathchair, with Mam, Bill and Dai as backdrop, proves that the family visited me at least once while I was in hospital at Ashurst. To avoid having to make any more long journeys to visit me, Mam somehow arranged my transfer to a Birmingham hospital. Normally, wounded soldiers had no say in the choice of hospitals. Still subject to military discipline, they went where they were sent.

I had been sorry to leave Netley, and now I felt very sad about leaving Ashurst. A move much nearer home, however, would sensibly reduce travelling for Mam when visiting me.

"Whenever you feel the urge to write," the senior sister in charge of the ward said, "I should like to hear from you. My home address is inside."

She handed me a present, a travelling writing case, then kissed me on the cheek and dabbed her eyes. The ambulance shuddered as the engine was started. We were off to Birmingham – to a hospital unknown to me.

CHAPTER 10

The ambulance entered Hollymoor Hospital, Birmingham, by a long, rising and curving drive. Dense shrubbery bordered the driveway: I could see where we had been by looking through the little square window set in each of the rear doors of the ambulance. The twittering of the young women in the front compartment ceased as we rolled to a stop outside the main entrance of the hospital. The rear doors were flung open and I was caressed with fresh air.

The sun was shining fiercely. Workmen, stripped to the waist, were busy cladding the fabric of the old building with filled sandbags. They were piling them neatly, in a running bond, up to about the ceiling height of the ground floor wards. I was not reassured by the sight of this defensive barrier since it implied that bombs were expected.

The hospital, a mental hospital, whose doors had also been opened wider in the national emergency, was barely a crow's mile from the Austin Motor Works, Longbridge. Now converted to making munitions, the factory was a prime target for enemy bombs and accordingly made the neighbourhood vulnerable to the overspill. Bomb aiming was so unpredictable that air forces were forced to indulge in stick bombing. Bombs were dropped one after another in the pious hope that at least one would hit the target. The sandbags would offer some protection from a meandering bomb landing near to the hospital but, if one landed within the perimeter of sandbags, the resulting explosion would be devastatingly contained.

My two exhausted female escorts delegated the task of unloading me from the claustrophobic ambulance to hospital porters while they themselves toddled off for refreshments. The frail creatures could expect to be fussed over for having navigated their vehicle safely over miles of unsignposted territory. The stretcher, on which lay a supposedly inanimate object, was dumped unfeelingly onto the hard, cool mosaic floor of the entrance hall. From this prone position I was able to see an intrepid duo being feted in a reception annexe. The rattle of hospital earthenware crockery suggested that tea and scones were about to be dispensed to those of us who were standing up.

I lay completely ignored for half an hour, timed by the clock on the opposite wall. It was a disdainful, institution-type clock that appeared coldly indifferent to the anxieties of its watchers.

An oldish young doctor in a tailored, unbuttoned white coat, the bridged ends of a stethoscope dangling theatrically out of a pocket, gazed down at me. His eyes then skimmed across me, as if he was looking for something he couldn't find. With a half-contemptuous smile on his creamy face he reached down for the medical file lying on the footless end of my stretcher. He flipped through the uninteresting pages and, without saying a word, dropped the file. Thrusting his hands back deeply into trouser pockets, he sauntered off. He had just passed, with honours, his random test in detached emotionalism.

The big hand of the clock swept fifteen more minutes of circular time. Two porters, both mute, possibly stricken in the same catastrophe as the phlegmatic doctor, carried me along wide, echoing corridors to a huge, high-ceilinged ward.

Commonly painted white, hospital ceilings ought to be decorated with murals for the benefit of supine bed patients who had to stare up at them for hours at a time. It would need an artist with the masterly horizontal technique of a Michelangelo, though, to paint this one.

The two, long and parallel rows of beds against opposite walls in the Nightingale ward were separated by a large expanse of the highly-polished wood flooring. My bed was anonymously in a middle of a row. With the help of a tetchy staff nurse I was rolled off my stretcher into it. The bedclothes were draped over me and tightly tucked in. Personal possessions taken out of my holdall were placed inside the bedside locker.

"We like to keep the locker top clear for medicines," the staff nurse said, trying to make an order sound like a preference.

"Now," she said, straightening herself, "would you like anything?"

"A cuppa tea?" I ventured, thinking she was thawing a couple of degrees.

"It will be tea time in – twenty minutes," she said lifting and glancing at the watch suspended from a formidable overhang of starched white apron. Her voice had the warmth of a railway station announcement. She rustled to the next bed, the restless patient having disturbed the bedclothes through not lying to attention.

Though back in Birmingham, the city that had adopted me, I felt lonely and yearned to be back in Ashurst Hospital. What made me feel sadder was the loving letter that had been waiting for me. It was from my woodland nurse companion, who was then on leave at her family mansion in Bournemouth.

I was confined to this big ward for two long months with just one brief respite when wheeled in my bed to see a spirited ENSA concert held in the hospital's main hall. The ward was a world of its own, remote from life outside its walls. The lawned gardens could not be seen through the windows above my head. The defensive barricade formed bays around ground floor windows restricting bed patients' views to that of the sky. Above the sandbags I could see the changing patterns of the clouds and could enjoy vicariously the freedom of birds.

One morning, Mr. Henry, a visiting orthopedic surgeon, entered a silenced ward. Heading the customary retinue of graded doctors and nurses he paused at pre-selected beds to discuss cases in solemn undertones with his followers.

He picked up my temperature chart and then consulted my medical file. Turning to me he asked me how I was feeling in such a kindly manner that I instantly took to him. He was a charming, friendly man. He did not look like a surgeon. Surgeons never do. Anyway, I had no idea what a surgeon should look like. After examining me, he said that he would be doing my re-amputations.

One Sunday afternoon, during the limited visiting hours, I was astonished to see the tall figure of Killer come striding into the ward. He looked along the rows, and then he saw me.

"You made it then, Cush!" he exclaimed with the sunniest of smiles.

"So did you. I never –"

We were engulfed in a welcome, both laughing, talking excitedly, asking and repeating questions and hardly waiting for answers.

We had both been wounded in that mortar attack during the battle for the Escaut River. We had afterwards lain cramped against each other on the open back of a fifteen hundredweight truck that carried some of the seriously wounded of Carrier Platoon out of Hollain. We were separated at the first casualty clearing station. I never expected to see him again; nor he me, as he now admitted with a smile.

He was still in khaki while waiting for his discharge from the Army. The bullet embedded in his head was extracted on his return to England. The operating surgeon was surprised to find that the bullet was 'one of ours'.

Killer said that he felt all right but confessed to being understandably prone to occasional severe headaches. Since then, I have run across Killer several times over the years when re-visiting Birmingham. Never once did I hear him moan about anything. He was always smiling, always cheerful.

No sooner had he told me what little he knew about others in the battalion when my Uncle Arthur entered the ward with Auntie Doris clinging to his arm. When they reached my bed, Killer gave me a swift look of puzzlement and got up from his chair. He stiffened himself before an immaculate groomed Army major who wore Air Force wings above First World War medal ribbons.

Two private soldiers, one stiffly vertical and the other inertly horizontal, were put 'at ease' by Major Yardley.

My mother's younger brother then asked me formally: "How are you being treated?"

"Very well, thank you," I replied to the clumsy question, ignoring rank or relationship because of my embarrassment.

"Good," he said, and Auntie Doris beamed down at me.

Equal in height to her husband she was, as always, stylishly dressed. They stayed just long enough for me to detect that my aunt had assumed a posh accent that had not quite ousted her Black Country twang. This was shamefully amusing to one himself not blessed with a dulcet-toned voice.

My uncle was an infantry sergeant in the previous war and had won his first commission on the battlefield. Shortly afterwards he had transferred to the newly formed Flying Corps, as it was then called, and qualified as a fighter pilot. Between wars he was a carpenter. When the Second World War broke out he had put aside his jack-plane, re-enlisted in the Army and was rapidly promoted to his present rank. Though he was not highly educated, having left school at the age of thirteen, he had done well in times of war.

He was a strange man, though, all on the surface. I never really knew him, or he me, for that matter.

I last saw my uncle just after the war at his rented home in a poor district of the Black Country. He blended with his depressing environment for he was shabbily dressed. Auntie Doris said they both had felt anxious about me when I was in hospital. That admission made me feel very sorry that I was not then able to help them financially. When my uncle died, penniless, the family rallied round to save him from being buried as a pauper. He had always struck me as being a sad, unhappy man and very reserved.

During my short stay at Hollymoor Hospital I did not form any lasting friendships. Though all the patients in the ward were service personnel, most of them were being treated for 'civilian' complaints so there were constantly changing faces. Only two patients had seen active service, a young, good-looking sailor, who was wounded while serving in the destroyer Ivanhoe off Dunkirk, and a Canadian fighter pilot who had a fractured leg.

The handsome, laughing matelot, when dressed in his uniform, shoregoing bell-bottoms, square blue collar and gold 'tiddley' badges, was a visual reminder of the distant seas.

The pilot raved, rightly but monotonously, about his Spitfire. He said that when flying his wonderful plane he could feel if there was a single rivet loose on it. Until, that was, a Messerschmitt loosened all of them in one go, forcing him to bale out of a doomed aircraft. On landing without it he broke his leg.

I had another unexpected visitor. He was a double amputee (above knees) of the First World War who sought those who had similarly lost legs in the Second. He was sincerely motivated in his self-chosen mission to encourage these others, especially the double amputees scattered thinly among them, to achieve his degree of personal independence. Since rehabilitation, the heavy jowelled man had become commercially successful. Happily married, he was bursting with self-esteem.

"We have a lot in common – heh! I'll see you again next week," he promised.

Sadly, my sunny visitor, who was hell bent on spreading his gospel, did not wear artificial limbs. He walked on pylons: short, round, tapered lengths of wood, hollowed out to fit his stumps and coupled together. He was just four feet tall and about as wide.

Unduly sensitive, and being saddled with too great a personal vanity, I knew I could not resort to that form of locomotion in public. His dreaded, repeated visits brought on moods of a deeper despair than that experienced at Ashurst. I longed to meet someone with identical high-up leg amputations who had been successfully fitted with artificial limbs. But I would never, ever do so.

Mr. Henry became concerned about me.

"I'm going to arrange for you to be transferred to a hospital in the countryside," he said, "where I also carry out operations. You'll find it a healthier place."

I was indebted to him for having me moved to my fourth hospital. He was a delightful man. He was always willing to discuss medical matters with his patients before talking among his retinue. He remained unaware that my progress had been halted by a well-meaning visitor with almost as high-up amputations.

Clinically, it was unfortunate that the fifth and last hospital where I was to be a patient was not the first and only one. That hospital not only specialised in amputating limbs but also in the fitting of artificial replacements. There, though still denied the encouragement of a direct comparison, I would undergo the postponed re-amputations with increasing optimism. Until reaching that last hospital, however, the uncertainties and doubts would continue to assail and gnaw at me.

Tony came to see me on his final leave before sailing for Canada, where he was being sent to complete his basic training. I met him in the main corridor. He was entering the hospital just as I was leaving it.

A tall, striking and wildly beautiful young auxiliary nurse, her cheeks pink through hurrying to come on duty, turned quickly on her heels when she realised who it was she had just passed in the wheelchair being pushed by an ambulance driver. In quick loping strides she joined us. She had a well-formed figure, wide blue eyes and blonde hair. The outspoken girl from my ward had noticed earlier that, due to depression, my confidence in myself had been ebbing. Typically, with her candid, warm-hearted approach to nursing, she had set about raising my jaded spirits.

Kneeling, she wished me good luck and then clasped me firmly and kissed me roundly for the last time. The adorable nurse left both Tony and the ambulance driver slack jawed.

CHAPTER 11

Several long, single-storey buildings at Barnsley Hall Mental Hospital had been commandeered for military patients. Mr. Henry had arranged my transfer to this war emergency hospital to build up my strength for what he had in mind for me. He left instructions that, after breakfasts, I was to be ejected from the ward into the fresh air.

The self-propelled wheelchair provided for this purpose was brand new. Every morning I patrolled the many paths of the hospital grounds in my new toy. The exercise in the cool, invigorating October air uplifted me and made me resolve to live to my full capabilities, however limited they may prove to be.

One crisp, bright day, after the morning mist had dispersed, I came across the hospital gardeners who, obeying the slogan, 'Dig for Victory', were preparing a vastly extended vegetable plot for late Autumn planting. It was their tea break and they sat on makeshift seats and upturned wheelbarrows.

A sage, as I found him to be, was sitting apart from the group as he rested from his double-digging and liming. We agreed about the weather, today's and in our predictions on tomorrow's. He probed delicately to see if an acceptance of a major disability had soured me in the process. He got me to agree, with little difficulty, that in spite of everything life was still sweet.

The clean smelling, newly turned earth had partially exposed an earthworm to pitiless daylight. A dignified robin, who had been watching the gardener work, was perched on the shiny shoulder of the upright spade. It hopped onto a dark clod of earth and claimed its territorial rights.

The worm clung tenaciously to the soil and strove to return to the safety of its dark habitat. It was stretched and thinned as the bird, straining on twig-like legs, eventually tugged it out. Holding the worm captive under restraining claws, the robin tore it into handy little pieces and shook them down. Dinner had arrived.

"Always remember, son," the leathery-skinned gardener advised, "you're still as good as the next bloke – but no better."

A hop, a brief flutter of wings, and the bird returned to its polished steel perch and rested from its exertions. After a while the robin's crown, above a bonfire throat, moved about in quick little jerks. Tiny bright eyes resumed an inspection of this part of a proclaimed territory. Its eyes met ours momentarily, seemingly associating us with an upturning spade and the tool itself with food. The bird wanted pudding. As if to express satisfaction with the service rendered so far, the perky songster broke into a repertoire of silvery notes that tripped over one another in an urgency of expression. The performance was accompanied by a shivering of wings and raising of the crest. We were brokenly serenaded for fully five minutes.

The old gardener, sitting on a ruck of bags of lime, was enjoying a mid-morning pipe. His mind elsewhere, he was looking at the robin pensively through a haze of puffed smoke that wreathed us both. I watched, too, smoking a cigarette, lit first from the same match. Yes, life was indeed sweet. At least, it was for three of four great and small creatures.

Then, with wry humour, the sage unconsciously summed things up for me, too, "Worms must turn," he said laconically as he knocked out his pipe.

The beds in my ward were jammed together in two opposed rows. The beds were separated by wedged-in lockers. The long ward, a wing of a single storey block, accommodated a friendly cosmopolitan bunch of lads. With very few exceptions they were there to be made potentially fit for active military service rather than being repaired after it.

Two of the patients were officers, an outgoing pilot and a normally quiet and reserved RAMC doctor. Both were young and were being treated for minor ailments. A rampageous padre visited the two officers every Sunday morning after he had presided over a nominal church service held in a hut. He drove the doctor's car and took the younger men out on a weekly, becoming ritual, pub crawl. Try as they may, the unsteady trio could not sing in harmony when they returned to the ward.

In the centre of our ward was a pot-bellied, cast-iron stove having a cylindrical chimney that disappeared through the ceiling. On cooler days, up-patients would stoke the fire until the pot-belly glowed a cherry red. We congregated around the friendly stove to listen to each other's reminiscences, mainly Gerald's.

Gerald had once served as an officer in the French Foreign Legion. He held us spellbound with his recounted experiences. During a posting to Indo-China, as it was then known, he said it was best to die by your own had than live to be captured by the enemy and then handed over to their merciless womenfolk. The 'gentler' sex would arrange a slow, cruel death for a captive. They would concentrate mainly on sexual differences as the life was being enticed out of him.

"We would never fire our last bullet in anger," Gerald said with a grim smile, "in case we needed some lead in an ear."

Gerald was the epitome of an English country gentleman. Tall, aristocratic-looking, he spoke in the cultured tones of those accustomed to receiving respectful advice from head gamekeepers. Yet, this was his first visit to the 'old country'. He was born in India, the son of a serving British Army officer. He had come to the UK to enlist. His one leg, badly broken when training, was completely encased in plaster.

Ambulant patients were expected to help the hard-working staff with their menial tasks. Jack, a stocky ex-pugilist, undertook to bath me regularly. I was not allowed to use a bathroom alone. I might slip and injure myself since there were no special handrails fitted in the spartan bathrooms. I was grateful to Jack. With the weaning off bed pans and now blanket baths a personal independence now looked to be attainable.

"Get your little rubber duck, it's bath time!" Jack would announce, a smile softening his hammered, rugged features. He wore a big gold signet ring. A gold letter 'J' was inset on the jet black face of a handsome ring that was considered to be impervious to soap suds.

Jack was deceptively strong for a small man. He lifted me out of my wheelchair easily and smoothly to lower me into prepared baths. This was no mean feat even though I weighed only seven and a half stones. Incidently, two whole legs – from the hip joints – are equal in weight to half the total weight of the entire body. My 'normal' weight, therefore, would have been at least twelve and a half stones.

My revealed, brutally abrupted legs did not repel Jack. His battered face never registered distaste for his self-appointed task. I felt that he must have been a great hearted little warrior inside a roped ring. Outside of one, I knew him to be a kind and gentle man. He would not divulge his professional name. He did not wish to be recognised or acknowledged, he said, so I did not try to wheedle it out of him.

Mr. Henry's surgical assistant, a young doctor, told me that I was making good progress and that I should be ready to have one leg re-amputated after Christmas.

"You don't want to be incapacitated during the festivities," he grinned.

"The re-amps will have to be done separately," he warned. "Be a two month's gap between the operations."

He was 'one of the lads' type of doctor, friendly and willing to chat. He found it amusing, on reading my medical notes, that I once had been fed on cherry brandy and delicacies. Now, I was on the ordinary, but adequate, hospital diet. It did not include much fruit, though, for it was in short supply during the war. Bananas, for example, were non-existent.

In spite of the transport problems Mam managed to visit me once a week, dovetailing her visits in between nightshifts at a huge factory in Small Heath, Birmingham. Always representing the family, she would arrive at the hospital on dark evenings and then rush back to her work on munitions. It was amazing how she stood up to it, visiting me in Bromsgrove, fifteen miles away, and working long night shifts. Nightly air raids on the factory, during which the workers would have to crowd into basements that did duty as shelters, added to the strain of it all. But it did not prevent Mam from keeping me supplied with toilet necessities and cigarettes.

Concealed, close to the hospital, was an anti-aircraft battery. It consisted of a battery of 4.7 ex-naval guns that had been elevated to point at the stars. Sited, presumably, to intercept enemy bombers making their inevitable nightly journeys to the industrial Midlands, they rattled our windows when thundering defiantly. A noisy, disturbed night would be followed by a tranquil morning and, looking northwards from the hospital grounds, distant columns of smoke would be seen curling lazily upwards to chilling skies.

On the night of 14-15 November 1940, Coventry suffered a hor-rifying mass air raid. Many inhabitants of the city died. Many more were injured.

Mr. Henry, along with other surgeons, was needed urgently to attend those victims rushed to Coventry hospitals for immediate surgery. Mr. Henry's health broke down under the strain of extra work and he himself became a patient in a hospital. During his absence from Barnsley Hall another specialist was to keep a weather eye on his stranded patients. Meanwhile, all non-urgent major orthopedic surgery at the hospital was suspended indefinitely.

I first met the dapper Mr Donavon about three years previously. He fixed my broken big toe. Later, after I had been turned down by the Army on medical grounds, he had examined me and suggested that I applied to join the Tank Corps rather than an infantry regiment. So, I stood accused of wasting his time on both occasions. Understandably, he did not recognise me: he would only remember 'cases'.

"Your stumps have healed nicely," he said after an examination.

He was making a clinical assessment of healed flesh not a cosmetic one.

"Unfortunately, he said, "your re-amputations will have to be delayed until Mr. Henry recovers from his illness." Turning to the absent surgeon's now serious-looking assistant he said: "Put him on traction."

Traction!

Traction, in my case, meant tapes and weights. Both stumps were individually and completely wrapped in surgical adhesive tape. Cords were attached to the looped ends of the wrappings. The two cords ran over separated pulleys fixed to the horizontal lower rail of the bed-end. Suspended on each tensioned cord was a heavy weight that yearned to sit on the polished wood floor. The intention was to pull – we have been down this way before!

After sampling new freedoms and a growing independence I found it irksome to be tied (literally) to a bed once more. If traction was such a good idea, why had it been discontinued after leaving Netley? Surely, it was too late now for it to be beneficial, and I was not old enough to have wrinkles that body stretching might remove.

The lads in the ward who had been, and those who had expected to be, temporary bed patients helped to relieve the tedium of one condemned to lay flat on his back. Whenever the severe-looking ward sister was off duty they gathered around my bed for extended card sessions, first having anchored me in an unofficial sitting position. We played for coppers and cigarettes. Nobody came away from the games rich, and nobody went without a smoke.

A young artist in the next bed to mine, who had been square-pegged by the Army into becoming a cook, gave me lessons in pencil sketching. He himself was brilliantly fluent with a soft-lead pencil. His hammer toes had been straightened to make uncompromising ammunition boots fit more comfortably. That operation was one of the last performed by Mr. Henry before he left for his Coventry assignment.

While in the expected supine position sketching and an

awakening interest in serious books, provided by kind (and optimistic) hospital visitors, helped me to put up with being stretched on my 'rack'. Now that Mr. Donavon had got his own back on me for wasting his time, for disregarding his advice and, finally, for having been careless, he left me alone.

The traction continued for three weeks. Then one quiet afternoon, the strict ward sister asked me if I would like to come off it. You bet! Mindful of a past painful experience, I opted to remove the welded-on surgical adhesive tape myself, carefully slicing through the hairs adhered to the tape with a razor blade. Jack ran a bath for me and, again, I was able to patrol the grounds in my nifty wheelchair.

It's a small world.

"How are you, Cush?"

The enquirer had been in my training squad at Budbrook Barracks, Warwick, and in my platoon, which had been formed from that squad, at Aldershot. I never liked him. Indeed, I despised him. He had proved to be completely untrustworthy and had been shunned by everyone in both squad and platoon. It is unlikely that he will read this, but if he did, it would be extremely unlikely that he would recognise himself. We do not 'see ourselves as others see us.' Nevertheless, his name is being purposely withheld, a distinction he shares with no other.

"O.K.," I replied in a low, uninviting tone that would have discouraged further conversation from anyone with a grain of sensitivity.

"Why are you here in Barnsley Hall?"

The question was wrung out of me by a guilty politeness. He was casually dressed in remnants of khaki. Obviously he was a fellow patient, but from a ward I had yet to visit.

"Gunshot wounds, left leg – Belgium," he chanted. "I've been here months. The leg has healed now. I should be discharged soon."

I had no wish to chat so I let him prattle on without interruption.

"With luck I shall soon be discharged from the Army, 'unfit for further military service', as they say. Then it's back to dear old

Brum for me."

"I heard that you had lost both your legs."

He was looking at me intently. His cold and expressionless eyes noted the empty space below the seat of the wheelchair. The blanket over my lap did not descend to the floor. If it had, it might get tangled in the wheels when I whizzed along the ward or patrolled the undulating garden paths at speed.

"You heard right."

I was gently prodding a sulking iron-pot stove into life. The ward had quietened into afternoon slumber. Our conversation was floundering. I suspected that he was up to no good.

"Would you like to go into Bromsgrove one morning? I could push you in that wheelchair."

A lock of his lank hair had fallen over one eye. He raked it back with his long fingers. He was weighing me up, coolly and without affection. His beaky nose rose up.

"If you sat on the top of that blanket, people will see straight away that you have lost your legs in the war. We'll be quids in – free beer in the pubs!" he said with an anticipatory grin.

"No thank you," I replied, glaring at him coldly, fiercely.

I could read then in his furtive face the realisation that he had not got away with it, this set purpose for seeking me. I resumed prodding the stove, but now more vigorously. I had to do something with the poker otherwise I would have brained him with it.

I disliked being detected in public as being obviously limbless, and over the years my feelings have not changed. I do not wish to flaunt my war wounds.

My visitor's blatantly insensitive proposal brought swiftly to mind my last trip in the wheelchair to the town. In descending onto a road from its pavement curb, the blanket draped over my lap fell off. Jack, who was pushing the wheelchair, knowing that I would stiffly resent being stared at by the understandably curious, rushed round and quickly retrieved the fallen blanket.

A middle-aged lady on the opposite pavement, who must have realised that we were from the local hospital, had sufficient time to note my disability. Pausing, just for a moment, she dashed across the road to me and thrust half a crown into my hand.

I felt as a beggar and deeply resented her spontaneous and charitable action. Reacting violently I made to return the offending silver coin. And then I saw that she was crying. My anger immediately subsided. Had she suffered a bereavement in the war? Without a word to me she patted my enclosing hand and walked by, head erect and with her eyes swimming in tears.

Illogically, I would cheerfully and readily accept a packet of cigarettes or a book from a hospital visitor. Perhaps my principles are unknowingly flexible.

(He's still here.) The thin, mean line of the spurned intruder's mouth had elongated to attempt something like a smile. Getting no encouraging response from me, he avoided my eyes and turned to go. The loose angular figure padded out of the ward, flat footed, as I had remembered him, but now with an added slight limp.

Ruth came to see me. On this, her first and last hospital visit, she was accompanied by an older sister. Ruth wanted confirmation how we stood with one another. While her sister was gazing discreetly around the ward Ruth agreed with me that we should break off our engagement. We parted on friendly terms and remained friends afterwards.

Her youngest brother, Len, whom I had followed loyally into the Army, was incensed when he learned that he was not going to be my brother-in-law. He wrote me a wounding letter from his station in India, a letter that obviously had escaped censorship. If ever we met up again, I could expect a fiery greeting.

Though Christmas, 1940, fell in an austerity period, it was celebrated in a joyful spirit at Barnsley Hall Hospital. There was enough to eat, a moderate amount to drink and a number of surprisingly talented patients toured the wards to provide entertainment.

My re-amps were, I thought, still scheduled to take place after Christmas. Afterwards I would be sent to Roehampton, London, for an assessment to see if I could be fitted with artificial legs. That is what I had been told.

However, owing to the continued absence of the senior surgeon there was to be an abrupt change in plans. Early in January the medical authorities decided to send me to a Leed's hospital that specialised in both surgery and the subsequent fitting of artificial limbs. The ward sister stunned me one evening with the relayed decision.

Next morning I was placed on a stretcher and slid into the back of an ambulance, something that was becoming wearily routine. It was snowing. The dull grey sky threatened a heavy fall. It snowed continually throughout the long journey northwards.

This time I had a travelling companion, a patient from another ward. A gunner of the Royal Artillery, he was a 'treble' amputee. His three main toes of one foot had been amputated and he was coming to Leeds with me for final stage surgery. Afterwards he could expect to be discharged from the Army. The quiet, serious Alexander was a devout Christian.

In the hurried departure from the hospital my personal belongings, in a gifted old suitcase, were left behind. The comradely young doctor from the end bed, who was discharged the same day, deviated from his long journey home in his car to deliver my scuffed suitcase to the nearest railway station. That kind act typified the helpful attitude of people during the war.

CHAPTER 12

As usual, I was not consulted about my transfer. It was the custom briefly to forewarn military patients of their imminent departure, put them in an ambulance and wave them off. Though no longer active in the Forces, we were still under its orders. So, I was sent to the Ministry of Pensions Hospital, Chapel Allerton, Leeds. It was to be my fifth and last hospital, at least it was as far as my war injuries were concerned.

Through the windscreen I saw a uniformed lodge keeper step out onto thickening snow to open heavy iron gates. After logging on his clipboard the admission of our ambulance into the hospital, he clanged the gates shut. His peaked hat drifted by each porthole window of the two rear doors as he returned to the comfort of his lodge. The grey day was darkening. From my lonely cabin I had a narrow, bipartite view of high walls and massive ironwork. It seemed a grim place. All that was missing was barbed wire and elevated machine gun posts. The ambulance stopped at the hospital main entrance. The engine was switched off and the chassis ceased shuddering.

'Alec', who had been riding up front to enjoy the views, disappeared to report to whoever just inside the building was on duty. The ambulance driver and his mate, who seemed to be reluctantly 'doing their bit', dumped my stretcher outside the main double doors and they also disappeared inside. The doors swung shut. Nobody came back.

The snowflakes fell, tumbling slowly. Then a sadistic wind

induced the snowflakes to swirl and to mask the fading light. The spinning flakes first speckled then whitened my covering red blanket and then threatened to obliterate me.

I recalled my delayed admission to Hollymoor Hospital, Birmingham. Then I had lain on a stretcher, forgotten, unwanted. It was a hot day, though, and the sun had shone brilliantly. Now, it was cold and it didn't. Night was quickly closing in. Soon it would be dark, very dark for no artificial light would be allowed to sneak out of the building.

Loneliness is lying on a stretcher on a gravel drive, at dusk, in a snowstorm, waiting for a hospital's uninviting big polished doors to open. Desperation is when they do.

Just before the low-lying stretcher and its frozen occupant became a hump in a blending white landscape, the heavy woodwork clattered noisily. Exactly one half of the timber swung inwards and was then wedged to prevent its automatic re-closing. The two bucolic ambulance men hefted me out of the crisp snow and bounced me into a haven of artificial light, warmth and familiar hospital smells. Evidently, my absent-minded attendants had suddenly realised, with a shock, that they were one short. My stretcher was placed on a trolley and the extra blanket of snow was swiftly, and not without a little embarrassment, brushed off.

A young nurse, who was small and perfectly formed, had been sent along that early winter evening to book both Alec and me into Ward 2 on the ground floor.

With a dazzling blue-eyed smile she said: "You're late! We were about to lock up for the night." Other staff members, who first met the double amputee, must have steeled themselves to meet the "treble".

Alec and I had been allocated adjacent beds in the big ward. He needed his only at night because he was an 'up' patient. He walked with a slight limp, which further treatment would virtually eliminate. Alec was a recent convert to Roman Catholicism. Every night, just before 'Lights Out' at 7 pm, he would kneel at the side of his bed and pray. You can imagine the ribald comments he generated from other military patients. The nightly asides began to peter out gradually until finally he was ignored as he gave thanks and sought guidance.

Our first day at the hospital began very early and in traditional style. The busy night staff brought round bowls of warm water for bed patients' token wash. Afterwards, pills and medicines were dispensed and beds were re-made. Those remaining in them were served breakfast by the ward orderly.

After breakfast, the day sister and staff nurse wheeled the agony wagon round the ward and attended to dressings. More pills and medicines were doled out.

Two staff nurses, having allowed their juniors a few beds start, rounded off the proceedings. Beds were re-made. Open parts of pillow cases made to face away from the door. Sheets were pulled taut over bed patients and then turned down just below chins and venomously tucked in. The movements of the mummified patients were then limited to shallow breathing. Abulatory patients sat dutifully and quietly by their beds in the reverently hushed ward.

Specialists, singly and in stages, and flanked by the surgical registrar and the ward sister, entered the ward to see their preselected patients on this weekly ritual. Housemen, staffnurses, and an auxiliary nurse carrying medical files, followed them respectfully. Once a visiting specialist had been launched into his prescribed orbit, there was no turning back, and no one dared speak unless invited to do so by 'his nibs'.

The orthopedic surgeon (stage two) to whom I had been donated was a mountain of a man whose spade-like hands obviously belied a surgical dexterity. Mr. Light would have a long and distinguished career. The relentless smile on his smooth round face would help to allay our fears and anxieties, before we were pollarded.

When I asked him that first morning if both my re-amputations could be done during one visit to the operating theatre so that the initial fitting of artificial limbs could be brought forward, his smile became indulgent. "I'll see," he said.

(He saw. They were done singly. I found out why.)

Lunch, the main meal of the day, was typical hospital fare,

nourishing but plain, unappealing and boiled. Sunday was always boiled chicken. Friday was boiled fish. Other main meals, though not tied to a specific day, invariably were cooked in saucepans.

After lunch, the hospital administrator, Dr. Richardson, did his weekly tour of the ward. He was a retired naval surgeon complete with goatee beard that made him look as the 'HMS Hero' sailor depicted on Players cigarette packets. A bright and cheerful man, he advised us about our future job prospects when we return to "civvy street". I told him that I wanted to be an engineer.

"While you're studying," he said, "find yourself a job as a cost clerk. It should provide a good grounding for an aspiring engineer. I started out as a cost clerk," he admitted surprisingly.

Later in the afternoon he returned to the ward carrying a surgical tray on which a hypodermic syringe the size of a cycle pump and some bright steel instruments clattered. A man in an opposite bed sat up, apprehensively I thought, and a nurse quickly arranged screens around him. Dr. Richardson spent about fifteen minutes in the temporary enclosure and then emerged holding his tray, as he had entered with it, horizontally and to his front. When the screens were removed the patient was seen rinsing his mouth.

Apparently the now shore-based doctor clung to one aspect of his naval surgery – dentistry. He offered a free service to captive patients. I hoped I should never need to suffer his raised foot on my chest.

The MOP Hospital was an artificial limb and appliance centre, a 'slave' to the principal one at Roehampton. The actual fitting of limbs was carried out in one of the huts dotting the grounds. Separated from the main building, these wooden structures had been erected just after the Great War as an urgent temporary measure. The legendary huts were proof that there is nothing so permanent as temporary.

During my time at Chapel Allerton (thirteen months) I would not meet even a near identical double leg amputee who had been fitted with artificial limbs, but I would grow more confident about eventually being fitted with them. I strengthened a resolve to try and overcome all obstacles as they presented themselves having witnessed tragedies that humbled me. Sadly, we are somehow uplifted on meeting someone we consider worse off than ourselves.

Like Netley, Chapel Allerton was an established military hospital. The patients wore 'hospital blues', bright blue flannel jacket and trousers, white shirt and flaming red tie. The dress was obligatory, even for ex-service men returning for further medical treatment. The deafening blue suits were washed frequently and always before being inherited by a new customer. They were comfortable to wear and were crease resistant. It was futile trying to knife-edge crease the floppy suit with a hot iron. Trouser legs would remain defiantly as two parallel tubes.

A wearer of these clothes in blazing patriotic colours was identifiable from afar as a patient of a military hospital and was therefore subject to its long-armed discipline. But the recognition would gain him free admission to matinee performances at local cinemas. It would also ensure his safe delivery to the hospital gates if, for some reason associated with a pub, he became incapable of returning there unaided.

The tight rules and regulations of the hospital had to be obeyed. Staff and patients alike suffered under them. The strict discipline descended pyramidically from the martinet of a matron: typically, a middle-aged spinster dedicated to a life of nursing. It descended to the ward sisters and to the patients; to staff nurses and to patients; to graded ranks of nurses and to patients; and to orderlies and cleaners who were on the same level as patients. Staff below the status of ward sister tended to exert authority self-defensively and self-consciously.

Most of the Second World War patients (I nearly said inmates) were, or had been, regular soldiers. Some of these men had been garrisoned abroad for long eventful periods. They now faced the prospect of a comparatively dull and pedestrian civilian life. The more boisterous among them found it hard to accept the restrictions of a walled-in military hospital.

The high walls that enclosed institutional buildings were not often softened with clingings of ivy. These grim barriers blatantly served a dual purpose. They had been built not only to prevent anyone on the outside of them from unlawfully getting inside, but, more importantly perhaps, to prevent anyone on the inside from unauthoritatively getting outside. Traffic either way was sometimes additionally deterred by pieces of bottle glass (noticeable in reflecting light) cemented in position along the top of a boundary wall.

The only official way out of and into the MOP Hospital, Chapel Allerton, was through the permanently manned lodge gates. When convalescent, we were allowed out until 5p.m., if authorised with a pass. A begrudged, and rarely issued, late pass would extend freedom a further two hours. Any infringement by a patient of the rigid rules would result in his pass being withdrawn instantly.

Sometimes, very late at night, crutches would be thrown over our high wall – the top of which had graciously been left unglazed – to land with a clatter in the quiet hospital grounds. A clambering, unsteady and merry-eyed leg amputee, who had become utterly bored with his confinement to hospital precincts after having his pass withdrawn, would follow his props.

As a bruised stump was being dressed by an irate night nurse the question would be flung at a comrade: "Why did you climb over the wall to get back in?"

The irrefutable logic of the pat answer defied argument and compelled admiration: "Because that was the way I got out!"

For a whole month I became a bed patient again simply because the only self-propelling wheelchair assigned to the ward was already being used by a soldier who had had a leg amputated above the knee. I acquired the wheelchair when he was discharged after being fitted with an artificial limb.

No one regretted his departure. A sour bloke, he had constantly bleated about his misfortune, the result of a barrack's room frolic with loaded rifles. Fortunately for him, his injury was benevolently defined for pensionable purposes as an acceptable accident. But he still felt hard done by.

The wheelchair was very old. It looked as if someone wearing a frock coat had simply attached castors and cycle wheels to an upholstered armchair. Compared to my last wheelchair it was an anachronism, but I was grateful for a cumbersome mobility.

Among the regular soldiers in the big ward was a quartet of self-contained, unsmiling hard men. Unusually, since it was a surgical ward, they were medical cases. Having been cured of whatever had ailed them they were now waiting to be discharged from both Army and hospital. Silently brooding, the clique played solo all day long on a light folding card table set aside for them. Allowed out on pass they would return with fixed hostile expressions that would repulse any attempts at comradeship by those not in the clan.

After 7p.m. ('Lights out') the foursome continued to play cards in the dimly lit lavatory, confident that they were unlikely to be disturbed in there. They bestowed upon me a special dispensation in tolerating a harmless infantile wit.

A middle-aged Lancashire man, a First World War veteran who had returned to hospital for treatment, taught me how to play chess. He was a very good player and I never learned enough to beat him. I was content to provide him with a bit of a challenge for he had a caustic sense of humour that appealed to me.

'Lanc' had been wounded in both legs which were now badly ulcerated. The ulcers stubbornly refused to heal and he had been warned repeatedly that they would not do so if he continued to swig beer at the rate he was doing. The final threat was amputation. Faced with that ultimatum Lanc compromised by reducing his consumption. The ulcerations did not heal, but they got no worse.

With a resigned air of acceptance he said to me: "It's stalemate with my legs, laddie – and this is checkmate, I'm afraid. But you're getting better!" he quickly added.

In a corner bed, at the entrance to the ward, was another veteran of Lanc's war, a spinal case who was permanently bedridden. No pillows to his bed, he lay completely flat. A 'driving' mirror was positioned a foot above his staring eyes. It was there solely to help him steer food into his mouth. When he became too weak to express himself audibly, the nurses learned to read the requests faintly etched on his drawn features. When he died, his visiting wife seemed suddenly to become frail and small.

Almost opposite me lay a suprapubic cystotomy case on a water bed. The young soldier with severe spinal injuries had been caught in an air raid while he was home on leave in Hull. His smooth skin was almost transparent through sickness. He, also, was doomed to die in that ward.

With very few exceptions the hospital's ward sisters were all approaching middle age, were spinsters, and were Irish. The previous war's incapacitated had been brought up properly by them over the years and knew what to expect if they did not toe the line. The younger patients tended to resent the dictatorial attitude of the senior nursing staff as if we were still in uniform. But we were still in uniform, and in a more colourful one. The auxiliary nurses, mostly conscripts, were similarly oppressed, but none of them would dare to raise even a resentful murmur.

All the staff worked long hours and were notoriously low paid, especially the ward sisters in view of their increased responsibilities. Living in the virginal seclusion of the nurses' home the sisters led the dedicated lives of nuns. On rare occasions their formal masks would slip allowing the perceptive a fleeting glimpse of their true selves. An unguarded moment would reveal an essentially good and kind person sheltering behind a stern exterior. I noticed this when the usually reserved ward sister told me, with a shy little smile, that she had added a seldom issued bottle of Bass to my daily diet.

On inheriting the ancient wheelchair I began to patrol the grounds, weather permitting of course. It was a refreshing change of air and surroundings. Coincidently, Nurse Doris Whitwham, who had admitted me to the ward on that snow-bound night, often took a stroll in the grounds before returning to her lodgings. She lived at the home of a local doctor. We began to meet regularly, away from the constraints of the ward.

There were park benches to sit on but none of them were sited to afford privacy. We sat together on each of the more secluded benches in nightly turns to deflect suspicion. We first draped a selected bench with my wheelchair blanket, then huddled together for warmth.

We spent many quiet afternoons in the ward when the sister was off duty. Ostensibly we were busy re-rolling washed bandages. We rolled thousands of them, or we should have done.

Dot, as she became to me, was a bundle of restless, impulsive energy. A shy girl, she held strong moral convictions given to be expressed with a flash of her remarkably blue eyes.

This strictly prohibited liaison of nurse and soldier had to be kept secret. My ward mates helped me to arrange the outdoor clandestine meetings with Dot. They would warn us of a threatening intrusion of privacy by whistling a popular tune. Normally, nobody in their right minds would feel like whistling in the grounds on dark, cold nights. It was therefore a signal that there was trouble afoot, or that a lunatic was abroad. On hearing it we had instantly to disentangle ourselves and part company. Dot had similarly involved her close nursing friends to whom she had confided her innermost feelings.

A suffocating ether mask drove me into a dreamless sleep and my first re-amputation was carried out. The stump was nicely rounded and showed just a neat, thin line of a scar under the bristling stitches. Swollen to about twice its previous size, the bruised stump was black shading to a patchy blue. It was extremely painful and the fiercest of phantom pains had been aroused. I realised then why Mr. Light had decided to operate singly. One at a time was almost too much.

It would be two months before surgery would be repeated on the other stump. It is amazing how quickly in ideal clinical conditions an amputated leg, or a re-amputated leg (virtually the same thing) will heal. Eight weeks after whichever operation, unless there are complications, the fitting process of an artificial limb could begin. My fittings, however, would be delayed to be paired, unlike the preliminary operations.

When my bruised stump had healed and shrunk to its normal size, I was allowed out again on pass. The weight of the wheelchair itself and the hilly roads in the district prevented my escort, a ward mate, and me venturing too far from the hospital. He and I shared three arms and two legs and these remaining limbs were fully exerted when ascending steep inclines. We were able to accept the kind invitations to afternoon teas from local residents. We did, just once, spend an afternoon together in a Jewish club. The members allowed us to play snooker but would not allow us to pay for our beers. The club was a long way from the hospital and we had to rush back in time for the five o'clock curfew. We were bushed, and that ruled me out for further visits.

My friend, the slim, good-looking John, had lost his arm through wounds received at Dunkirk while waiting on the sands to be evacuated. His arm had been amputated at the shoulder, consequently the artificial replacement limb made for him had no practical use since he had nothing to operate it with. His non-functioning arm was therefore rarely worn. Anyway, as he would point out, when solo he frequented back street pubs and low dives in the city, he felt safer with a flat jacket-sleeve thrust into a redundant pocket. He reckoned that, when seen as obviously disabled, he would be less likely to be picked on.

I gave the customary royal waves from my trolleyed stretcher to left and right rows of well-wishers as I was wheeled out of the ward to the operating theatre. There I was presented to a waiting Mr. Light for my final re-amp. This time unconsciousness was induced swiftly and not distressingly by a new method, a pre-injection of pentothal. Trustingly, I expected to return, after surgery, along the same route. I should have remembered: I had no say in these matters.

CHAPTER 13

The world in which I slowly regained consciousness began to assume an unusual form. I was in a strange ward: one on the upper floor, it transpired. The pre-planned separation of nurse and soldier had been made without first informing either of them. My antiquated wheelchair, which had been sent along to comfort me in my loneliness, looked strangely out of place in these new surroundings. A nurse, whom I didn't recognise, offered me just a cup of tea because she knew that I would be feeling too sick to eat.

That night Leeds suffered an air raid. A small bomb wasted its pent up energy in making a hole in the hospital drive. During that sleepless night my stump began to haemorrhage through the stitches. I was taken back to the operating theatre, given a whiff of gas, and the needlework was re-tightened.

Alec came to see me the next evening. "I've brought your toast," he said.

We had taken turns to make it in the small kitchen of my old ward when the day staff went off duty. He handed me a note from Dot.

"I'll wait for your answer and give it to her when she comes on the ward tomorrow," said my Christian-minded friend.

My heavily swollen, pain-generating stump kept me in bed for some weeks. During this inactive period the Army decided to get rid of me. My discharge, though inevitable, was premature and hatched in a curious, unfeeling way. It left me wondering why the authorities could not have delayed my discharge from the Army for just one day, or until I became an up patient again. I had spent fifteen months in hospitals, would be a patient here for at least six more months, so what did one day matter? One week? One month? To me? To the Army? Rhetorical questions that find no answers from the officers who tetchily hurried the discharge of a private soldier.

The impressive-looking Certificate of Service red booklet issued to me contains the following entries:

Military Conduct
Very good. Qualified by his conduct to have received an award of 'EXEMPLARY' for Military Conduct, but ineligible because he has not completed three years service.
Length of Service: 2 years 364 days.

So I did not earn the Exemplary Award, whatever it was. But I was Honest, Sober and Trustworthy, as were most all discharged regular soldiers.

Early in the war, honourable discharge from the Army was covered by old, peace-time regulations. There were no gratuities and no demob suits. A discharged 'other rank' could either keep his greatcoat or receive £1 instead. I opted for the money having mislaid my greatcoat in Belgium along with other accessories of war. We were allowed also to keep one pair of our ammunition boots. I lost my last pair when I lost an argument with a trench mortar. Anyhow, I had nowhere to put a pair of boots at the time, and when there was somewhere to put them, I needed a smaller size.

Medals were distributed after the war. Illogically, the Belgium Campaign was the only campaign of the war not commemorated with a star. That is why I was awarded eventually only two medals, the War Medal 1939-45 and the ubiquitous 1939-45 Star. Some people got a row of medals for simply turning up. However, if my two were awarded to me on the basis of one for each missing limb, then I ought to feel grateful that I had not qualified for a chest full.

2   (This page should be entirely free from erasure.)

Final Assessments of Conduct and Character on Leaving the Colours.

Military Conduct _Very good. Qualified by_
Testimonial _his conduct to have received_
an award of "EXEMPLARY" for
military conduct, but ineligible
because he has not completed three
years service.

However, sober & trustworthy.

The above assessments have been read to the soldier.

Signature of Soldier ~~on~~
~~Transfer to Reserve~~
or on Discharge
(Delete words which are inapplicable.)
    F. Adam.

Place _Warwick_   _John Nicholson Capt_   Signature
and Rank

Date _10·7·41_   O.C. 03/6 Records

Service with the Colours shewing Transfers, if any, to other Corps.

Corps	Country	From	To	Length of Service	
				Years	Days
R. Warwicks R	Home	6.8.38	19.9.39	1	45
	France	10.9.39	15.5.40	—	248
	Home	16.5.40	4.8.41	1	11
				2	304 1/4

3

When this last bout of pain and swelling had subsided I took stock: both stumps were now nicely rounded, almost naturally so. No scarred flesh visible, just thin red lines where the stitches had been. Both were far better looking than the carrot-like below knee amputations of the lesser disabled. I would say that, wouldn't I? It's true, however.

Now kindly avert your gaze while I move aside the naughty bits and position the tinned end of this linen tape into each groin. Inside leg measurements are now:– Left: 6 and ³/₄ inches (say, 17cms.). Right: 6 inches (say, 15cms.).

A single amputee having a short stump and fitted with an artificial limb has to rely heavily on his good leg to drag around the other when walking. Having none of the original issue left, I had to face the daunting, but challenging, prospect of lowering myself into a brace of coupled artificial limbs and then hoping that I could drag both of them around. A spur, if needed, would be the shocking alternative, those short lengths of tree trunks...

Allowed out again, I arranged to meet Dot at the homes of local visitors to the hospital. Joe, my new helpmate now that John had been discharged from hospital, pushed me along to these discreet trysts, usually at the home of the Klegermans, a poor and kind-hearted Jewish family.

Joe Jarvis, like his forerunner, had only one available arm. A dispatch rider, he had survived Dunkirk intact. At Bristol, where his unit was re-mustering, Joe was blown up during an air raid. His injuries included a paralysed left arm. This injured arm was now rigidly encased in an 'aeroplane' splint in a horizontal position, slightly bent at the elbow and stretching outwards from his side. It was hoped that the severed nerve ends in his static arm would eventually knit together. The dark-haired Yorkshire man was very tall so we didn't have to duck so low when he turned round suddenly with a scything movement.

Our meetings were not kept secret for long. The hospital lodge keeper, a Mr. Hobbs (inevitably dubbed 'Jack'), who had seen better and more disciplined days, reported to the matron a suspected defiance of the regulations. That put the tin lid on it.

Once involved, Matron's reactions to this sort of thing going on in her domain moved on light waves. Dot was summoned to her office early next morning and given half an hour's notice to collect her personal belongings and ordered to report for immediate duty at another Leed's hospital. Simultaneously, the hospital administrator had been advised to withdraw my pass.

Sister O'Halleran, back on duty and first doing her round of the ward to enquire about our day's health, broke the news to me after I had replied automatically: "All right, thank you, Sister. "

She leaned forward. "I'm afraid, Cottam, your pass has been withdrawn," she whispered.

I was sitting in my wheelchair and sketching from a photograph. "Why?" I asked dumbfounded.

'Killarney' now had my full attention. On learning that her first name was Kate, we called her by this alliterative prefix when she was out of earshot.

"Perhaps it has something to do with Nurse Whitwham's transfer," Killarney suggested, dropping another bombshell. Her fresh, unblemished complexion had deepened in still greater contrast to the dazzling whiteness of her starched bib apron.

I was stunned. Dot transferred! I a prisoner!

Aware of my amazement and sorrow Killarney said, "Cheer up. Seacroft Hospital is not very far from here. Nurse Whitwham should be able to come and see you now as an ordinary visitor."

That was a novel suggestion!

Again erect, she said primly, "Behave yourself and I'll see what I can do about getting your pass restored."

She turned and asked my neighbour, Patterson, "And how are we feeling today?"

Patterson was a professional engineer in civilian life. Small and compact he was a few years older than myself. His perpetually worn glasses gave him an owlish mien. He had one leg off below the knee and was waiting to be fitted with an artificial limb. Meanwhile, he humped about on crutches. Meticulous, precise, his daily routine was governed by his Rolex watch. He relaxed with Rothmans hand-made cigarettes – sent to him by his parents. He lit them with his Ronson cigarette lighter. Of Rolex, Rothmans and Ronson we others had none.

In Killarney's eyes Pat was a model patient, a gentleman who broke no rules so they did not have to be repeated to him. Unwittingly, he set an example to the rest of us in the ward. When she spoke to him, or about him, it was noticeably in a softer tone of voice. That apart, he was a helpful companion.

He had refuelled the desire to uplift myself educationally and I had asked him to teach me grammatical French to reinforce a colloquial knowledge of the language. Knowing that I aspired to become a member of his profession he said his time would be better spent helping me with a subject related to engineering.

"Mathematics is the basis of all branches of science and engineering," he propounded. "You should study mathematics."

So be it. 'Gig Lamps' had spoken.

He started to teach me maths, beginning with algebra. Killarney allowed us to use the dispensing room, which was opposite her office in the passage way leading to the ward, as a schoolroom. There, early evenings, Pat set me on my chosen path. The sister seemed proud to be associated with the venture, possibly thinking that there was still hope for Cottam.

Dot now lived in at the nurses' home of her new hospital and was able to visit me regularly, wheeling me out when my pass had been restored. We planned our future wedding while sitting besides each other on a prominent bench in the hospital grounds. The cheery Dr. Richardson saw us seated together one day.

"Good job you didn't lose your arms, Cottam!" he shouted.

Dot and I became engaged. Dot was just twenty-one. I was exactly two months her senior. I had found the money for the engagement ring and Dot bought me an inscribed gold tie pin out of her miserly pay as a nurse. Our plans were hatched optimistically because we did not know how I would cope with artificial limbs. If unable to master them, it would be very difficult to find a suitable job. Without a job I should not contemplate marriage. The full disability pension due to me, though an indisputable 100%, would not properly support even a bachelor.

Dot, however, never wavered in her love for me – and she would not ask for the moon.

Dot was accustomed to working long, staggered hours in return for poor pay. At the age of thirteen she was found a job as a house maid at a doctor's residence, near to the MOP Hospital. Village girls were assumed to be fodder for the domestic service market and Dot had been permitted to leave her village elementary school a year earlier than anticipated to start work. Dot was put in the care of an old housekeeper and taught to cook to sew and to wait at table. It gave Dot an insight into a gracious style of living: the young doctor and his fashion-conscious wife, a childless couple, regularly hosted dinner parties at which black ties were worn.

Following a spell as the doctor's surgery maid, Dot trained as a nurse, first at St. James Hospital, known locally as 'Jimmys', and then at the MOP Hospital. Until being transferred to Seacroft Hospital, Dot had stayed at the doctor's house though she was working elsewhere.

Dot's home was in a coal-coloured mining village, north of Doncaster. The house was at the end of a terrace in a euphemistically named 'Spring Street'. Her father, having escaped from the pits, still worked for the mining company that reigned over the village. He was a slater and odd job man, employed to repair miners' homes. Like his daughter, his wife had also been in domestic service when young. Dot had no sisters and just one brother, who was nine years her junior. As a child Dot was encouraged to be infant Tom's constant young mother. The encouragement came in slaps. That enforced relationship would stifle, until later years, the natural sisterly affection for an only brother.

Though I had still to meet Dot's parents, I felt that Dot and I could expect opposition from them if we decided to marry. Conversely, I suspected that there would be opposition from my single parent if we didn't for she then would feel saddled with a social misfit.

On entering the ward one afternoon for a late turn of duty Killarney began her usual round. As always she was immaculately

The author, Eric Cottam

The author's future wife – Dot Whitwham

dressed. White, wide-flowing cap that allowed only a frontal wave of gingery hair to show, white collar, pressed light grey uniform and white bib apron. The sleeves of her uniform were now buttoned down with starched white cuffs, not rolled up and held in position with white, ruffled elasticated cuffs since surgical dressings had been completed for the day. Elegant, tallish, straight-backed and estimated to be about forty years old, she was cleanly attractive in predominantly white.

She glided into the path of my wheelchair and then stood quite still. Her sensible, shiny black shoes were pressed together. I drew up. Her hands were clasped over the big silver buckle of the 'Lonsdale Belt' denoting her nursing grade.

Bending slightly forward she said, less formally than expected and with an anxious little smile: "How are you today, Cottam?"

I sensed that, this time, the routine daily enquiry about the state of my general health was merely serving as openers.

"Quite well, thank you, Sister," I replied – and waited.

"I wonder –", the soft brogue faltered. She made another attempt. "I have to ask you if you would do something for us?"

I saw an elephant trap opening up before me for she was embarrassed and was trying visibly to arrest her feelings. When not objectively nursing, renewing surgical dressings, removing stitches or attending emergencies, she was always a little ill at ease with her patients and wary of being lured into polite chit-chat with them. The request, which had made her blush slightly, was therefore something unusual, and something that already had triggered a recent soldier's defence mechanism reminding him never to volunteer for anything.

"We have a new patient in a side ward downstairs, a paraplegic," she continued gamely. "He's a pilot officer – and very ill," she said in a lower tone.

Her grey eyes under sandy eyelashes met mine. It was my turn to feel embarrassed. What she had said, or rather, the way she said it, was tantamount to admitting that the man was terminally ill. Killarney could not, would not dwell further on his condition.

"Would you care to pop down and have a word with him? After

144

tea, say, when he's been made comfortable for the night?"
So that was it. Would I mind comforting a dying man!

* * *

"Have you been sent along to cheer me up?"
The voice was light, cool and clear. The slightly raised head was small, round and outstandingly boyish. Only the school prefect's cap was missing. His complexion was pale, but he did not look seriously ill; a little tired, a little too bright-eyed perhaps, but certainly he did not look as if he was about to die. I braced myself.

"No," I countered, trying to sound convincing. "I saw the open door and thought it should be interesting talking to a fighter pilot. I have a younger brother who is aiming to be one. Also, I could bore you with my troubles, assuming, of course, that you would care to listen." I grinned encouragingly.

A disbelieving smile lifted the corners of his mouth. The penetrating eyes in the implausibly young head mirrored a swift intelligence.

He laid aside the paper back he had been reading and asked me politely, "Why are you in hospital?"

His view of me in that cramped, one-bed side ward was restricted to my head and shoulders.

"DAAK – double amputee above knees – Belgium."

"That's why they sent you!" he announced with a grin.

"Nobody sent me," I lied, grinning with him and gaining confidence. "We are a friendly lot here. You would not be aware of that being isolated in a side ward because of your officer rank."

"That's true. It hardly matters, though I was only brought to this hospital for a short stay. It is much nearer to my home than my last hospital and my parents can visit me here more often. You see – I am going to die. I have only a few weeks left to live." The voice had subsided.

"I can't believe that!" I exclaimed, upset by the unexpected confirmation.

"You shall," he said with conviction. He showed no self-pity.

145

I was shocked, out of my depth, silenced, not only by the news, but by his calm acceptance of it. He was resigned to the fact that he was going to die – and soon! He did not sound bitter about it, nor did he seem fearful of a so untimely exit from this world. Unable to converse on this level, I listened attentively as he told me about himself. I hoped to hear something that could be viewed as medically disputable, something on which I could hinge an optimistic argument. I did not. He was going to die.

He was an only son, an ex-public schoolboy, and younger than myself. A Hurricane pilot in the Battle of Britain he had been shot down by a German fighter plane. There was a big hole in the middle of his back. The terrible wound had robbed him of all bodily feeling below it.

He had a quick and lively mind. It became apparent that he had read widely. Reading was now his only occupation. Despite the grim outlook he had retained a sense of humour. The book I had disturbed him reading, and to which my own reading had not extended, was Stephen Leacock's *Literary Lapses*. He read aloud extracts from it and we laughed together.

On a later visit he told me with vicarious pride that his much more experienced squadron leader would often close to within fifty metres of an enemy plane before pressing his firing button. He, himself, in similar situations, had seldom got closer than one hundred metres to a target. Even at that greater distance, he had seen an opponent's goggled face, he said.

It was astounding how that young fighter pilot had come to accept with such great dignity that he had so little time left on this earth. It was humbling, yet uplifting, to share some of it with him. How could I ever feel sorry for myself? Had Killarney tried to ensure that I never would?

One late afternoon, after seeing Dot to the hospital gates, I decided to pop in and see my pilot friend (I never knew his name – we had only exchanged wounds) before returning to my ward. For the past three weeks I had been visiting the little side ward regularly.

In the lower corridor I ran into a tearful and unseeing middle-aged couple, evidently his parents. I was saddened by the implication. A feeling of inadequacy prevented me from intruding upon their grief. Slowly, and sadly, I wheeled myself to the lift and returned to my ward. Killarney met me in the passage way

"I have something to tell you, Cottam," she said softly in her Patterson voice.

CHAPTER 14

As they were not able to visit me on my twenty first birthday, my family sent me presents by post. Patterson described them, unkindly, as burnt offerings. Closing ranks, I pointed out to him that all three were working six long shifts a week in munition factories so they hardly had the time to visit a distant hospital.

One Sunday, about a month later, my mother and younger brothers, Bill and Dai, did visit me. They could spend only a few hours with me on this belated visit as they had to catch the last train back to Birmingham. Dot was on duty at her hospital that day and could not get time off to be introduced to my mother and brothers.

Bill was now studying for the RAF preliminary examination for aircrews. When eventually he passed the exam, he donned a blue uniform, a better one than Tony's. Dai, who then was eighteen, volunteered to wear a khaki one, as I had done. He topped his, though, with a red beret.

That Sunday, after my mother and brothers had left, a Great War veteran was admitted to our ward for immediate surgery. Brown was a ghost of a man and just as silent. He had a German sniper's bullet lodged in an inaccessible place in his stomach region. Twenty-five years after being shot he began to suffer increasingly from stomach pains. Surgery had become imperative. The bullet had to be extracted or he would most certainly die.

Next morning Brown walked lopsidedly to the bathroom. He returned to his bed, still without speaking to anyone and put on a white enveloping operating gown. The exertion of pulling on the long white woollen stockings made him wince with pain. He lay back on his bed and waited patiently for the ward orderly with his trolleyed stretcher to take him to what would become a peaceful, pain-free death on the operating table.

Burgoo, our ward orderly, was an ex-guardsman. He was nicknamed after porridge because that was how he greeted us, first collectively and then individually, every morning: "Burgoo! Burgoo?"

Tall and lean, his rugged handsomeness was fading. His Brylcreemed hair was swept back in the lateral waves of a 1920's matinee idol. A genial, talkative man he had an enormous sex drive, so he would have us believe. Burgoo freely offered the physically handicapped on his ward, which meant most of us otherwise we would not have been there, his unsought advice on how to remain athletic in the bedroom.

"You will have to encourage a greater participation," he would suggest in more basic terms, his craggy face registering a grinning optimism.

The long awaited day arrived!

I was summoned to the Artificial Limb & Appliance Centre. Once inside the hut, I found the startling became gradually to look commonplace. The hut was cluttered with artificial legs of many types. Among them, amputees were putting on or taking off their metal limbs. Dismembered limbs, propped up in odd corners of the wooden building, were labelled with names and reference numbers to identify the absent wearers.

The chief limb-fitter introduced himself to me and simply admitted: "We don't get many like you."

A veteran of the previous war he himself was limbless, a single-leg amputee just above the knee. He had expertly adapted to wearing an artificial replacement and walked better than anyone I knew with a similar disability. He walked with just a slight suggestion of a limp. He could run, too, if not quite so fluidly, confirming the suspicion that he who walks with a limp will very likely run with a hop. He had been seen running to board a tram as it groaned its way up the hill near the hospital gates. He was an inspiring character who didn't get very many like me.

"Not very many," he continued to exaggerate, "but I feel sure we can do something for you. You're young and fit. That's in our favour. But you have very short stumps so we must not expect too much too soon. It will take time and we shall expect your full co-operation. With perseverance we should have you walking eventually on artificial legs".

That was the most heartening news I ever had and I was just about to ask: "When –?"

"We must face facts, though. Don't be misled into thinking that you'll become another Bader. You won't. Both your stumps are very much shorter than his one off above the knee. His other leg was amputated below the knee. I once refitted him, you know, while I was at Roehampton."

"Back in a minute – put your jacket over your shoulders. Must not catch cold."

I was left perched on a firmly padded high bench seat, which was situated at one end of the fitting room. Men, single above and single below knee amputees, were walking up and down in various states of undress. Their thin-metal artificial legs were bared for inspection and adjustment by attendant limb-fitters.

Some of the amputees were aided by walking sticks, but not all. One that was had a leg off well above the knee and he walked with his artificial replacement kept stiff, knee lock on. He clicked it off to sit down. A similar amputee walked slowly up and down between a long length of hip-high parallel bars, easing his way between the supports. He walked with an emphasised knee-straightening action followed by a hip sagging motion. An eagle-eyed fitter, kneeling at one end of the bars, watched his patient intently.

A few of the limbless I recognised as fellow patients of the hospital. The others were mainly ex-service men from the last war who long since had been integrated back into civilian life. They were being refitted with new limbs or having repairs and adjustments made to their existing limbs, sometimes both.

There was only one double amputee on parade. A bank

manager who had lost both legs below the knees. Stripped to singlet and underpants, to allow quick access for inspection, he was walking up and down the long room – perfectly and without using a stick. Apparently he was a passably good ballroom dancer.

One man, sitting nearby, had removed his bright metal leg having satisfied himself, and convinced his limb-fitter, that it fitted comfortably and that it would not cause undue soreness when next he wore it. He put his old leg back on and then the clothes he had taken off. The new limb, he told me, would be returned in its raw state to Roehampton, where it had been made to order, to be finished and spray painted an unbelievable flesh pink. Years later, regulation assertive pink was superseded by an unassertive buff colour.

He told me about an Army officer serving abroad in a hot climate who specified that his artificial leg sent home for repair be left unpainted because brightly polished metal would reflect the sunlight making his limb cooler to wear when playing tennis. His limb was returned to him elegantly burnished.

(Recently I heard of another odd case: a coloured girl who had refused to sign for her new artificial leg because it had been spray-painted black to blend with her natural colouring. She complained that she was being discriminated against and insisted that her limb be resprayed the standard buff colour, as were the artificial limbs of all white patients.)

The chief limb-fitter came out of his office holding a medical file. His alternate harder steps resounded on the bare floorboards.

"I've had a word with the medical officer he said," raising his voice to be heard above the cacophony emanating from the partitioned-off workshop next to his small office. Bench hands were hammering to reshape sheet metal and their noises had risen to a deafening crescendo.

"We have decided," he said, again adjusting his voice during a momentary lull in the noise from the workshop, "we have decided to restrict you to a rigid pelvic band on your pylons – and your limbs," he added swiftly on noticing my crestfallen expression. "That's being technical. You'll get to know these terms after a while. First, we'll measure you for pylons. You know what they are, don't you?"

Downcast, I admitted that I did know. "Yes, they are little wooden supports –"

"Right. We'll get you walking on those to slim down your stumps. Nothing unusual about that. We sometimes fit a new single above knee amputee with a peg leg for the same purpose to save the expense of having to refit a proper artificial limb."

He began his measuring. "When you have mastered the pylons, we shall re-measure you for limbs. They are now made of metal, not wood, so we are no longer able to keep our socks up with drawing pins," he joked.

I felt less despondent as he took measurements and entered them in the medical file. He then took plaster casts of both stumps.

That completed, he asked abruptly: "What colour would you prefer your pylons to be?"

I fumbled the unexpected question. "Does it matter? They are only for temporary use in here."

"Well –" he hesitated. "You may decide to use them occasionally when you get home."

Was he being pessimistic – or realistic? It was not uncommon for high-up double amputees to remain on pylons after first learning to walk on them? Was he hedging his bets?

I stalled. "What colours are available?"

"I would suggest a mahogany finish," he said with a hint of finality.

That ended my first, and illuminating day at an artificial limb and appliance centre. The overall impression that remained with me was of amputees being for ever dependent on sheet metal workers and limb-fitters for their mobility.

A month later I was recalled to the limb-fitting hut. Chief came to me as I sat on my perch expectantly. He was dragging along my two pylons. Steadying himself he held them up for my approval. My mind was then more willing to accept the new and the novel than it is now, but I viewed that which confronted me with a mixture of disbelief, anxiety and gloom.

Externally the pylons were mirror images of each other. Each 'leg' was about 18 ins. (45 cms.) long and 8 ins. (20 cms.) diameter tapering to 4 ins. (10 cms.) and had been lathe turned from a log of wood. They were finished in a rich mahogany colour except the last 3 ins. (7.5 cms.) of their blunted ends, which were black and nicely capped with round rubber soles. The tops of the pylons had been bored out and shaped to suit the replicas formed in my plaster casts. These inside surfaces were lined with chamois leather. The outer top edge of each separated pylon was linked to half of a leather-encased stainless steel pelvic band by a pivotting stem. One had to admire the superb workmanship.

"Put these stump socks on," Chief requested producing two white woollen hats without bobbles. "They go up in numbered sizes, by the way. Both yours are the smallest: size '0.' Remember that when you apply annually to the Ministry for double re-issues."

Placing the pylons on the floor he held them steady in an upright position. Two young fitters hefted me off my high bench seat and lowered me into the woodwork. The halves of the pelvic band were laced together at the back and buckled at the front. Wide canvas braces, similar to those worn by parachutists, were attached to the back of the pylons then draped over my shoulders to be anchored at their fronts. My entire body weight was now being supported on the rims of the pylons. I weighed, it seemed, at least forty stones.

The two fitters, each holding up one of my hands, walked me the length of the hut: Clomp, clomp! Clomp, clomp! At this very far end, screwed to the wall, was a tailor's mirror. We paused in front of it to allow one of us to have a breather before he was about turned. I stood splay legged on my wooden supports between hand-holding attendants. I measured four feet nothing in two directions but I felt quite tall.

After a dozen or so clomping trips up and down the lengthening hut I became sore in the groin. Also, the blood had drained from my held-high arms. Unaccustomed to being completely vertical had made by back ache.

Chief called time. "That's enough for today," he said and I was dismantled.

The next day, though sore and stiff, I was impatient to get back on my pylons in order to graduate quickly to proper artificial limbs.

"Try these," Chief said when I had been assembled and harnessed. He handed me two standard-issue walking sticks that had been cut down to half their original lengths.

Unaided by the escorting two fitters, I made it to the mirror and took a hard look at myself. The image of an oddly proportioned midget attempted to dwarf me in spirit. The short substantial figure, the disarranged telescoped clothing and the shortened sticks reminded me of a clown in a tented sawdust ring of a circus.

Resolving to regard the wearing of pylons as just a phase in my rehabilitation and to make light of it, I straight-faced asked the fitters: "Where are the buckets of water, the plank and the step ladders?"

Within a week I had learned to walk without sticks – I hadn't far to fall, anyway. Then I began to run slowly, if it could be defined as running. To lift up one pylon to place it forward I had to rock over stiffly onto the other because of absent knee joints. This shuddering, hip-rocking action limited my speed when in overdrive, so I walked fast, or ran slowly, with a blurred outline.

To avoid having continually to crane my neck I talked to people's midriffs. Being unique, even there, I overcame a feeling of slight embarrassment by fooling about, erratically staggering around the hut.

Dot and I were now meeting and corresponding regularly. Dot had spoken to her parents about me. Understandably, they did not share our joy when they learned that their only daughter was engaged to be married to a severely disabled man. They were hard-working, down-to-earth people of solid Yorkshire stock and had hoped that Dot would marry a village lad.

Assessing me as a smooth-talker with no job prospects, Dot's parents, mainly the mother, went on the offensive. Whenever Dot returned home for a week-end break, mother and father would spend hours with her until late at night trying to convince her of the folly of our association.

Blithely I continued walking daily on my pylons in the hut, describing my progress to a rebellious daughter. I had noticed that the sparkle in her blue eyes was dimmed, and that her ready smiles were tinged with sadness after she had spent a couple of days at home. Her subdued moods puzzled me because I was not told about her parent's objections to our plans. Her mother would one day enlighten me.

A young patient in the ward had a car. A medical case, he had a full complement of limbs. The car was an old Austin Seven that belonged to his father who owned a small garage in an outlying village. On Sunday mornings, providing we had scrounged enough petrol to mix with available supplies of paraffin from Dad's garage, he would take me to his home. First stop would be his village pub.

"Carry him in quickly!" he would demand of his two impressed helpmates. "He doesn't like to be seen uncovered."

Two or three pints later we would visit his rickety cottage and eat a splendid traditional Sunday lunch, Yorkshire pudding followed by the roast beef and vegetables, prepared by his attractive young wife. Afterwards, while I lay in a drunken stupor on the settee downstairs, he and his wife would disappear upstairs. The silent room would begin to sway, and the shaded light suspended above by head would, too, but it would do so independently, rhythmically.

Back to the hut. Two snow caps of dried plaster of Paris were removed from my rounded stumps. Chief picked up my medical file.

"We have decided to make you five feet eight inches tall on your artificial limbs," he explained. "Your 'normal' height we estimate to be now nearly six feet – you've grown a little since you were injured. Anyway, we always 'reduce' double amps. to lower their centres of gravity – it makes them more stable on their new legs. The compromise shouldn't make you look too tall in the saddle," he promised after relaying the decision.

Five feet eight inches seemed a reasonable height. Dot was five feet three inches. We should photograph well on our wedding day.

" – I remember fitting a guardsman – last war double amp, mid-thigh. He had been six feet seven inches. Even though he had been very tall originally, I should imagine that he had had unusually long legs – I only meet people when they've lost them. We 'made' him six feet. That's the one advantage of fitting double amps. No such flexibility with single amps. We have to match the lengths of artificial legs to natural ones, and match feet."

"Feet!" he said, suddenly reminded of something. "What size feet would you prefer?"

"Don't artificial legs have feet attached to them?" I asked deadpan.

He sighed and brushed back a wisp of grey hair and gazed at me sorrowfully yet kindly. Resisting a playful impulse to strike me with the medical file he said patiently, "Of course they do, but their actual size is decided here. Now, what size were your feet before?"

"Size eight."

"Right, let's agree on size seven for your new limbs, shall we? It should be in proportion. Rigid pelvic band, rigid joints..." he mumbled to himself as he filled in the form.

I reported for pylon duty every week-day morning while waiting for my full-length legs to be made at Roehampton. I was overjoyed at the prospect of becoming life-size again.

One quiet afternoon I sat in my wheelchair and gazed idly out of a window at a grey day. The view from that elevated ward window was depressing. Heavy raindrops had started to dance on the paving slabs below and pools were forming on sunken surfaces of the tarmac drives. Sodden lawns, with growth suspended and the bare black fronds of the petrified trees standing on their single legs in stark simplicity gave notice of impending, harsher wintry weather. Massive black clouds began to scud across a sky of dark grey and the rain began to pour torrentially.

Most bed patients were sleeping off a leaden midday dinner. Joe had offered to take me out for a breath of fresher air, but I suspected that it might rain. The upholstered wheelchair would absorb water like a sponge and then squelch it into me. I just hoped that it would be dry the next day when Dot would be visiting me.

A hollow echoing of footsteps on the polished wood floor grew louder as a nurse approached. She rescued me from dozing saying, "You are to report to the limb-fitting hut straight away. Your artificial limbs have arrived from –"

I left skid marks!

I undressed and a fitter hung my saturated clothes over a radiator to dry. I examined my new legs. You will have seen an assembled suit of armour in large entrance halls of noted stately homes. Usually, the tin suit is partly hidden in the well under a soaring staircase. Steel hands are frozen in the air; the vizor is down to quietly suggest occupation. My bare, coupled and unpainted artificial limbs looked just like the lower half of a suit of armour.

The swivelling stainless steel pelvic band was covered temporarily with a stiff canvas sheath. The band itself would have to be uncovered for re-shaping to a perfect fit around my hips. The tops of the thin metal sockets had not been nicely rolled over since the sockets themselves were bound to need beating to a better fit. Stiffened rolled edges would hamper adjustment. A push rod, side-mounted below a pelvic band swivel joint, operated that leg's knee lock.

Chief and an assistant helped me into my new limbs and then harnessed me by linking the wide braces back and front to the twin roller cords that ran internally over each knee pivot. Chief warned me not to allow the stump socks, which curled over the sharp-edged tops of the sockets, to fall down the holes: "If that happens, the sharp edges of the metal will seriously endanger your medals."

New shoes, size seven, were prised onto my feet. It is almost impossible to walk properly on a pair of artificial legs without footwear once the angle of the feet has been set to accommodate a depth of heel. When erected to a standing position the braces were fully tensioned. I felt strange and light headed at five feet eight inches and grateful that I could now look directly at people.

Supported along my way, I made it to the parallel bars. I walked stiff-legged, as if on stilts, between the bars, up and down, up and down sweating buckets. It must have been easier learning to walk

157

when an infant. Granite determination was needed as well as a stiff upper lip.

High spots in the sockets began to chafe me. The legs were removed and, while I rested, bench hands coaxed and smoothed sheet metal. Then it was up and down and up and down again.

Channelled by the parallel bars I walked daily on my bare metal legs. Minor running (inapt word) adjustments to sockets, pelvic band and angle of feet were made frequently. After a week of this activity the limbs were returned to Roehampton for finishing. Meanwhile, I kept in trim by trotting around the limb-fitting hut on my mahogany pylons.

CHAPTER 15

While waiting for my artificial limbs to be finished I should like to compare, in a practical way, the different type of leg amputations, beginning with the least reduction in the length of a limb. Syme's amputation of the foot through the ankle joint had become a rare operation. It resulted in the patient being fitted with an odd and cumbersome surgical boot. Surgically, it was found preferable to amputate the leg about seven inches (17.5 cms.) below the knee. This less troublesome stump could later be fitted with an artificial 'leg' that would allow a free choice of matching footwear.

The loss of a knee is a greater handicap. The future agility on an artificial leg of an above knee amputee will depend mostly on just where the thigh bone now ends, the longer the stump the greater the leverage and therefore stability on the new limb.

An entire leg amputated at the hip is a very serious handicap. An artificial limb made for the unsightly 'stump' involves ankle, knee and hip joints and is familiarly known as a tilting bucket, after its type of socket. This appliance is very uncomfortable to wear and often is stored at home in the loft, the owner having returned to his faithful crutches.

There is general agreement among leg amputees that one off at the hip is a far worse disability than two off below the knees, virtually the loss of two feet. It is even worse, in my opinion, than one off below the knee and the other off above the knee, if this last mentioned case has been fitted with two artificial limbs.

In future years I would associate with many limbless people, but I would not meet among them anyone who had lost two legs completely – that is, disarticulated at the hip joints. A survivor of that double amputation would not be seen at an artificial limb-fitting centre.

One arm and one leg double amputees were not uncommon at Leeds. Usually the limbs were missing on the same side, the one that had received the main force of the blast, or whatever had caused the joint injuries. It is debatable whether this proves to be comparatively less of a handicap than if the amputations had been diagonal (opposite sides).

The foregoing layman's analysis of leg amputees and of their artificial limbs sums up what I had learned at Leeds. I learned also that single amputees were provided with two artificial limbs and double amps, four, in pairs. This was necessary to maintain the limbs in good repair and in case the sockets have to be re-fitted due to physical changes in stumps, sometimes reflecting alterations in body weight. The lengthy process of refitting could then be under-taken singly enabling amputees to remain mobile.

My new limbs arrived back from Roehampton. They had been spray-painted a flesh pink and their sockets, with lips nicely rolled over, perforated like a colander. Bright metal parts were chromium plated. The rounded feet (no individual toes) were covered in chamois leather. The steel pelvic band was encased in new leather. New, heavy duty, blue canvas double-ended braces were draped over the limbs ready for coupling to the twin round leather roller cords of each limb. Roller cords were in pairs in case one of them should break.

With the aid of two full-length walking sticks I walked, with a heady triumph, up and down the hut slowly. Though aware of my possible limitations, I was elated by the fact that I was now able to walk again. Psychologically, it was tremendously uplifting.

Walking with artificial limbs would always be at a comparatively slow pace, particularly when doing so with one knee bending naturally. Polished floors, mosaic and tiled floors when damp, cascading steps of public buildings, greasy pavements, high curbstones, icy roads, steep inclines and rough terrain were to prove hazards best circumvented if confronted with them.

I soon found that, generally, it was better to leave both knee locks on and to walk stiff legged as if on stilts. It makes me even more conspicuous in public, but I am less likely to fall over. Better to be embarrassed than bruised.

Nowadays, leg amputees are encouraged to wear the new suction-type of artificial limbs that dispense with pelvic bands, braces and roller cords. This improved method of anchorage has just one drawback. Should a vacuum collapse, a limb could be jettisoned, and that would be inconvenient for the wearer if amusing to onlookers. Because of the extent of my amputations I am considered as not even remotely suitable for this newer type of limbs. I have, however, progressed to white nylon braces and sun-tanned legs.

I signed for this first pair of artificial limbs and shook hands with Chief.

"You will be measured for your second set of limbs at your local centre in about six month's time." His face then creased into a triumphant grin. "I shall now confess," he said, "you are the highest double amputee I've fitted with artificial limbs instead of just pylons. The best of luck to you."

The pylons, incidently, were re-lined and followed me home. I never again wore them, not even indoors, and certainly would never have had the courage to wear them defiantly outdoors. After the pylons had been tucked away for some years I was given Ministry permission to convert them into mahogany yule logs.

Next morning I assembled myself and sat down at the ward dining table for my up-patient's breakfast. My hospital blue trousers were unfolded to their full length and I looked as normal and complete as the other fitted patients around the table, AKs and a BK. Only Joe, sitting opposite to me, looked obviously disabled in his primed readiness to deliver a left hook. He was soon joined by a leg and arm case, however, who unplugged a gloved right hand and inserted the handle of his knife into a blunted bright metal wrist. The blade of the knife protruded eerily from an empty sleeve cuff.

Joe cut a bit off his single rasher of bacon, rotated the blade of his Nelson knife – named after England's saviour – and forked it. His loaded knife halted before his open mouth. "We ought to celebrate your first full day on your legs, Eric. Shall we go out and have a drink after I've done my stint?" he suggested. "We could tell Killarney that we shan't be back for one-o'clock dinner."

"Good idea! I'll drop a line to Dot to let her know that I've got them and then I'll take a little walk outside. How are we fixed for money?"

When I returned to the ward Joe had finished damp-dusting and tidying top shelves, a task entrusted to him because of his height. I got into my wheelchair and we arrived at the Queens Arms precisely at opening time.

The wheelchair was necessary. Long walks were to prove energy sapping, particularly the return journeys when often it was realised that I had swam out too far. I was already sore that first morning through breaking in my new limbs. Strictly speaking, the unyielding limbs were breaking me in. Just sitting in them was becoming uncomfortable. It was like being tightly strapped in a steel corset. Continually wearing the limbs would harden me to them.

Though chafed and cramped in my restricting metal-work, I insisted on standing in the smoke-filled bar rather than remaining isolated in my wheelchair and having a glass handed down to me. Fully erect I was no longer an attraction for the maudlin and garrulous who were inclined to stoop and shout down my lugholes when I sat in my wheelchair.

The bar was comfortably occupied by a gaggle of 'generals' in mufti who were becoming critical about the way our leaders were conducting the war. Their brilliant grasp of strategics should have been made available to the War Cabinet when the pub was shut.

The future, as I saw it in the smoke haze, was rosy. Standing upright in public for the first time in nearly two years had boosted my confidence. I drank in celebration and the future became rosier. Leaving the Queens Arms we wheeled our way to the Mexborough Arms. We left the comfort of those Arms to enter someone else's Head.

Finally emerging into the bitingly cold air the alcohol we had poured liberally down our gullets unleashed its stupefying effects. We laughed inanely and sang raucously off-key in an attempted duet. The unmusical duo was well and truly Oliver. Joe pushed the wheelchair and in return it supported him. Late that afternoon we weaved through the hospital gates and charitably wished the lodge keeper, Hobbs, who looked dourly on, a premature: "Merry Christmas, Jack!"

Turning into the drive leading to the main entrance we ran slap bang into an immovable mother-in-law elect, who, it seemed, had been waiting impatiently for me. I sensed right away who she was when she rose from the park bench opposite the lodge. She stood formidably in our path like a Pennine boulder, the personification of the indomitable English spirit in rock form.

A little taller than Dot she was heavier, wide-hipped and matronly. Plainly dressed she wore an unfashionable, good quality hat that looked as if it was moulded to her head. Both gloved hands held the strap of a leather handbag. Her demeanour was compounded of defiance, resentment and hostility. Metaphorically and literally there would be no way of getting round her.

Young Tom, with a half-anxious, half-listless expression, clung to his mother's coat pocket. His eyes darted from Joe to me then back up to his mother's stern face. He, too, was startled when she spoke.

"Are you Eric Cottam?" she growled in a gruff, uncut Yorkshire accent.

Her colourless lips were tightly pursed in disapproval. Though both Joe and I were now 'legless' the enquiry was aimed at the one sitting in a wheelchair seeing that he had at least two good arms.

"Indeed I am," I replied in an elevated Brummie accent.

"You cannot marry my daughter!" she exclaimed without preamble. Compressing her lips had tightened the fierce expression on her oblong face.

"Why not?" I asked finding sobriety slipping away from me again now that the shock wave of the sudden confrontation began to ebb.

"You have not a job for one thing, and little chance of getting one," she sniffed.

Obviously, she had made this bleak assessment from what little information about me she had prised out of her unconfiding daughter. The remark stung and made me to look at her more closely.

Her face, lined and careworn through years of domestic drudgery, had long ago abdicated any pretensions to beauty. Her straightened hair was two shades of grey. Her teeth were not her own. Under my rude stare her face had flushed.

Reluctant to bandy words with her, I did not explain that I intended to carve out a career in engineering. I felt that she would not believe me. Faintly detecting the anguish that had driven her to find and face me, I tactfully remained silent. In any case my personal problems had been pushed further aside at each pub Joe and I had visited.

Joe was leaning over the back of the wheelchair trying to get some response out of a bewildered Tom when Dot's blunt-speaking mother made her memorable request: "Let me see you walk!"

Unfortunately, that day's spell of walking had been done. I was sore and wanted to get out of my restricting limbs. Furthermore, I had drunk too much and would have had difficulty in just standing. My balancing mechanism had developed an insidious fault – shumfing was wrong shumwhere. Ma, as she became known to me in much more friendlier times, had as much chance of seeing me walk as she had of seeing Joe play a trombone.

Dot was embarrassed then furious when she heard that her mother had visited me uninvited. On sober reflection, though still smarting from her forthright manner, I realised that Ma had descended upon me out of concern for her only daughter. I told Dot this and then clasped her to me for she was shyly happy at seeing me standing for the first time.

A group of young limbless ex-service men, who had recently been fitted with artificial limbs, was taken from the hospital on the back of a hired open truck to Leeds University. There the various types of amputees were paraded, in turn, before a medical assembly. I got star billing, but it was not because of my agility on new limbs – my comrades were athletes in comparison to me. Our Dr. Richardson, who led us in turn onto the stage, presented me as an extreme challenge, and as a successful mechanical reconstruction.

We recall joyous, magical moments along life's way swiftly and dwell upon them sweetly. Christmas Day 1941 at the Ministry of Pensions Hospital, Leeds was, I flatly recorded, followed inevitably by an equally unexciting Boxing Day.

CHAPTER 16

The issue of a meagre ration of clothing coupons, the sartorial equivalent of ration coupons, had allowed me to add a lounge suit, two shirts and a few underclothes to my civilian wardrobe of one pair of shoes. Self-consciously tricked out in bland civvies, I said goodbye to my friends wearing flamboyant hospital blues.

Joe would remain in hospital for many more months before it was decided to amputate his useless arm at the shoulder. Like John, from whom he willingly had taken over the job of wheelchair prime mover, he would wear a non-functioning artificial arm for dress purposes only.

Escorted by my mother, I was taken by car on a very cold morning in January 1941 to the snow-swept city centre of Leeds. A worse day could not have been imagined for my re-introduction into civvy street. Apparently the whole of Britain was snowbound, but this would not be confirmed in the newspapers or on the radio because the classified information might be of use to the enemy. Though assisted, I had the greatest difficulty walking just the short distance to the station because of the unadmitted crunching snow on the pavements.

The railway carriage was crowded. People with determined expressions were noisily moving along the corridor frantically seeking unoccupied compartment seats. Soon, as it became evident to the seekers, there were no seats available. The disappointed stood resignedly in the passageway and stared vacantly at nothing. Jammed together were men no longer young, women of all ages and some members of the armed services.

Mam had earlier commandeered the last two seats in our compartment and had steadied me into one of them. My small suitcase, containing all that I owned, and my new walking sticks (Ministry issue) she had placed on the sagging network of the luggage rack above our heads. We settled back into moquette-covered seats that smelled of stale tobacco and prepared ourselves for a slow train journey, with frequent stops, to Birmingham. Squashed together, we all withdrew into our private worlds.

Pretending to be admiring the beautiful paintings of towns and villages underneath the opposite luggage rack, I thought about Dot and of our forthcoming wedding. On the way to the station Mam had readily agreed with me that Dot and I should get married as soon as it could be arranged. Killing stone dead any romantic notions I thought she might have harboured, she had said flatly, "In your position you may not get another chance to marry."

A personal vanity, which would not acknowledge a great physical disability, saved me from a lasting hurt. I recalled that Mam had never really fallen in love with any of the men she had known. Not to have done so may account for her hard outlook on life. She was wrong, however, in thinking that I would marry out of desperation, or that I would do so to shed her of a supposed responsibility.

I was excited about returning home. Surreal and powerful memories of Warwick, Aldershot, France, Belgium and of the five hospitals, where I had spent a total of twenty months as a patient, reeled through my mind. The memories would grow warmer as I experienced the harsh reality of domestic life in wartime Birmingham, which made me then realise that I had been living in comparative luxury. My bed and board had been provided and I had had no responsibilities. I had not endured regular nightly air raids in this country. Now, I would have to live and work in Birmingham as the Germans strove to blast the pulsating heart out of it.

I should be able to find a job because of the war. The choice of jobs would be limited, though, since I was fit only for factory work. Ironically, I would be returning to where I had escaped from on joining the Army.

Among those standing in the corridor were two whispering women with sullen expressions. They were looking askant at the young man wearing a smart grey herringbone suit who was seated. They seemed to be suggesting that he ought to offer one of them his seat. Moreover, why wasn't he in uniform?

The train moved slowly as if weighed down by the packed humanity that crammed every compartment and the corridors. Frozen suburbia flashed across the window. The blinding whiteness of a thick blanket of snow covered the fields and creviced bare black trees. It was overcoat weather but I could not afford one until I had saved enough money from my weekly war pension, when it came through.

We arrived home in the afternoon. Home, now, was a three-up and three-down, semi-detached council house on a sprawling, soulless estate on the edge of an expanded Birmingham. The family had vacated the old fish and chip shop in bomb-damaged Balsall Heath just before the whole row of shops was flattened by a land mine. In this fairly new house lived my mother, brothers Bill and Dai and, not surprisingly, a lodger, Patrick. The Government preached to householders that it was their duty during the war to take in lodgers, but Mam had long been converted to sharing her homes with them.

Bill was now at his diminutive physical peak. He was a positive thinker with a good brain, but one that I personally have never been able to key into. Dai promised to be the tallest of the brothers now that I had been reduced in height.

My, later our, bedroom was the downstairs front room. It was furnished simply with a three-piece bedroom suite and matching bed in dark oak veneer – a wedding gift from my mother. Before the intrusive furniture could be installed in an empty room, Bill had to reassemble his motor bike and vacate his indoor garage. The bed handily concealed from view a confessed irremovable oil stain on the bare floorboards.

Excusably, the rest of this house, like our other homes, was poorly furnished. Inexcusably, it was dust layered, dirty and had lacked applications of soap and water. The chipped and abused furniture was starved of polish. A whimsical approach to house-keeping coupled with a Bohemian outlook on life had always soon reduced every one of Mam's new homes to a state of confusion and disarray.

An internal door, which had separated the hall from the living room, had been removed, as was testified by two hinges hanging lifelessly on the stark door frame. "What happened to the door?" I asked Bill.

"We were cold," Bill said enigmatically, and he smiled his usual sour smile.

Coal, like other fuel, was strictly rationed. Suspiciously, there was a supplementary supply of wood by the open fire in the living room. The pieces of wood tantalised me into trying to jigsaw them into original shapes.

I put my few things away in the chest of drawers and sat on the bed. It struck me that I had to adapt to live here. Organised life in orphanages, the Army and then hospitals had left their marks on me. I had to suppress feelings of contempt before the acceptance of adolescence came back to me.

"Eric!" Mam said softly, breaking in on my dizzy thoughts.

She stood in the doorway for a moment, then came in a little awkwardly. "The lavatory and bathroom are upstairs, I'm afraid," she said. "Think you can manage to climb the stairs? There is a banister."

"I'll try to. Otherwise I shall have to take my legs off when things become urgent and crawl up the stairs to – what's that racket?" Young female voices could be heard chattering, squabbling.

"Dai's bloody harem! Look out of the window."

A row of girls was sitting on the low wall that separated the front garden from the pavement. They began to yowl for Dai – Daviiid! – to join them.

When he did, they practically fought over him, their savagely applied vivid lipstick getting smudged as they brawled. Though available young men were scarce, and though these girls led empty lives on a drab council estate in dreary wartime, this adoration of my youngest brother simply amazed me. I would no longer resent being told that we were lookalikes.

"It would be a great help if you would become chief cook and bottle washer while the rest of us are working," Mam said. "Dot can take over the job when she arrives."

Start adapting, Eric.

I had been home a week when a voluntary welfare worker called to see me. He was a retired business man and a geographically remote friend of Mrs. Ross, who lived in Leeds. When I was in Chapel Allerton Hospital Mrs. Ross had benevolently 'adopted' me and regularly brought me food parcels. She evidently was following this up by asking her friend to call and see me and to let her know how I was coping at home. He reported back loftily about 'unsatisfactory living conditions' and that he could be of no assistance. I replied to the anxious letter from Mrs. Ross and thanked her sincerely for her past generosity and added that no help had been sought from her friend.

I was not overly worried about the state of the house. It would provide a temporary home for a thankful, newly married couple. Once Dot and I had found our bearings, we would look around for a place of our own to rent. Dot, due to arrive next month, might think differently about staying here, even temporarily, on seeing this dump. A strict upbringing followed by domestic service had instilled in her good housecraft. Her instant reaction on seeing from where I had sprung would be my last hurdle to overcome.

Inadvertently, Dot's blunt-speaking mother came to my assistance. When she did leave home to marry me, Dot was given a traditional warning: "You've made your bed – you can lie on it!"

That, then, was home. It was similar in many ways to the one I had left to join the Army over three year's ago. During that time I had learnt a little and had acquired a physical disability. When sent to a Leeds hospital because of that disability, however, it was my good fortune to meet Dot.

Dai and Pat both worked long days in factories. My mother and

Bill were also on munition work, on long night shifts. Industrially, Birmingham never slept on those dark unlit nights.

Early mornings I had a meal of sorts prepared for those who had just finished work and for those others who were about to start. Afterwards, my mother left the table and retired to her bedroom with a companion cigarette.

Bill, the other night-shift worker, slept downstairs. He went to bed only on Sunday mornings, knowing that he would not have to get up later in the day to go to work. Evidently, if he had gone upstairs to bed after finishing a shift on other mornings, he would quite likely sleep through his next shift because he was physically exhausted through overwork. Knowing that wartime mobilisation of all available labour had made absenteeism from work officially displeasing, Bill sat, all day, in a hunched position, on the lift-up seat of the left hand fireplace-fender box in readiness for his next shift. Mesmerised by flickering flames, he soon fell into a deep sleep, and that is understating a fact. Single-minded Bill never did anything by halves. He did not merely sleep. He would fall into a coma to become almost moribund.

His loose-fitting, belted camel coat was always left on. Long folds of the worn and faded cloth draped perilously near spluttering flames when Bill ascended to his astral plane, where he would remain oblivious of earthly dangers. Overlapping scorched patches on the lower reaches of his long coat, which trailed on the 'LYON'S TEA' enamelled hearthplate, indicated the number of times he had put himself at risk of dying red hot. "See that he doesn't fall in the fire," I would be requested by a weary mother.

My job description included the task of waking up a mother and one son for a night shift. Waking up Bill, and telling him why I had done so, demanded perseverance and a thick pelt. Bill had an evil temper which tiredness accentuated.

Every deathly quiet morning I prepared selected vegetables for the late dinner and relaid the table. I was then off duty until nightfall. The whispered news emitted from the 'gold inlaid' fret-worked fascia of the domed wireless set offered little hope of the war ending the next week. The slimmed-down daily paper was soon read. So, while Pat and Dai were at work, and while my mother slept and while Bill emulated death, I read the books I had begun to accumulate.

The wispy net curtains at every window in the house were backed with a light-absorbing heavy curtain to comply with the strictly enforced blackout regulations. These matt black, curtains would suck up light and crush it when drawn tightly at dusk to allow no escaping lines of yellow round their edges when a room was dimly lit by single suspended, half-shaded sixty watt bulb. At night, the unattractiveness of the living room was blurred by the dim lighting and the mellowing open fire. Stark daylight, however, cruelly exposed the shabby condition of the fireside chairs and the battered appearance of the dining room suite. The cracked lino and the poor decorative state of the dreary room contributed to an atmosphere of defeat, which contrasted with the coloured wedding portraits of Mam and Dad in oval mahogany frames who gazed triumphantly across at each other from opposite walls.

I could not venture outdoors. A premature thaw had churned up virgin white snow and reduced it to grey slush on the roads and pavements making walking hazardous even for agile people. The nearest, and small, shopping centre was almost a mile away and I had no means of getting to it. In any case, I had very little money and every conceivable thing was either strictly rationed or in very short supply.

Shops opened at irregular hours, sometimes imperiously, and on to queues. Shopping had lost its attraction for most people during the war, but, if a queue began to form outside a retailer, it became advisable to join it, even if at first not knowing what was about to be dispensed.

I was confined indoors for a several weeks because of the bad weather and was therefore able to be a constant guardian angel to Bill, who sat on a fender box with his chin on his chest. The twinned 'antique copper' fender boxes, incidently, were similar to those I had assembled at one factory where I had worked when a youth. That is why they are so easily remembered. He who sat on one of them is also unforgettable.

You may wonder why he chose to sit there rather than in the more comfortable fireside chair opposite mine? And why didn't he remove his overcoat? Being nearer to the fire guaranteed warmth. Wearing an overcoat made him less likely to be affected by the sly, searching draughts introduced through a missing, sacrificed door.

A charity, concerned with occupational therapy for hospital and ex-hospital patients, sent me sample materials, leather, felt, silks, canvas and wool and with them a promise of a starved market for my future products. I would earn a cut of the profits.

In one hospital I had occupied my unlimited spare time with leatherwork. In another I made felt tea cosies. At Leeds I embroidered. Now, though, I felt that I ought to be aspiring to greater things. But I was marooned amid streets of slush and a mile away from the nearest bus stop. I opted for leatherwork. It seemed a more masculine pastime. I made ladies' leather handbags.

My mother seemed to resent my hobby, as I preferred to think of it. "You've been busy again," she would grumble, not comment, on returning home and noticing a previous day's output.

Perhaps she was worrying about getting permanently saddled with me. We had never discussed matters seriously, deeply. Now, it seemed impossible to bridge the gap between us for our conversations had regressed to an interchange of simple statements.

Dot was disheartened, predictably, when she saw the state of my family's home. My prospective mother-in-law's impending visit for the wedding, and her expected reaction on seeing my home, caused Dot more anguish. Dot's forthright mother obeyed the injunctions: "Cleanliness is next to Godliness" and "Speak as you find." Straight from the shoulder stuff.

During the weeks before the wedding, Dot set to every day cleaning up the place. Late at night, after a full day's cleaning, washing and now cooking, she would leave, as arranged, to sleep at neighbour's house.

The neighbour was an overflowing lady in kindness and size. She had a regularly-spaced, great number of children and her poorly furnished home was spotlessly clean. The unpolished dining table top had been scrubbed that often its grain was ribbed and raised knots in the wood had become hard and knobbly. Where lino had failed to reach skirting boards the exposed floorboards were scrubbed clean, as were the bared stairs to the bedrooms. The contrast confirmed an opinion about our house.

When the weather improved we hired, at a weekly charge, a Tan Sad folding push-chair from a city hospital and Dot took me out in it. Our first outing – and it felt as if I had been released from prison – was to the local vicarage to arrange the wedding. The smiling, old vicar greeted us warmly and took us into his library. The muted and sedate room had an air of permanence. One wall was impressively and completely lined from floor to ceiling with books. A curtain dust sheet had been withdrawn a little to one side. A sliding ladder, hung on a rail, provided access to the higher-placed books.

The scholarly vicar, when taking down particulars, asked me how I became to be disabled. I told him, briefly. He then generously waived the church fees for the wedding. As Dot often reminds me, I got her for nothing!

Dot yearned for a traditional white wedding. Being hard up we could not afford the cost. The whiteness of our austere wedding was provided by the snow-covered landscape. There was no organ accompaniment and no ringing of church bells. We could not raise the organ fee and the ringing of church bells had been banned for the duration of the war, except to signal an invasion. Dot's wedding outfit was a powder blue two piece with burgundy accessories. The flat, monochrome wedding photographs do not do her justice and merely highlighted the Brylcreemed hair of the younger males.

After the quiet ceremony, strains of my relations from Staffordshire soon departed. We congregated only at weddings and funerals. Duty done, there was no point in hanging about. Dot's parents stayed overnight at our motherly neighbour's home. They left early next morning to catch their train back to Yorkshire. They left with an air of having attended a funeral.

Eric and Dot's wedding at Yardley Church, Birmingham on 21st Feruary, 1942

Now that we were living together under the same roof, Dot took over my domestic duties. It was a thankless and frustrating job: responsibility without authority.

Night air raids began to intensify. In the suburb where we lived there was only one attractive target for German bombers, a big munition's factory. Occasionally it was singled out for special attention.

Dot and I were alone on the night of our first raid. The sirens began to wail. When they continued to wail, the rising and falling warned us what to expect. Dot carried me down to the shelter and then returned to the house for my artificial legs. They were an integral part of me now.

We sat in the domed, corrugated-iron shelter, which was covered with earth clods, and heard the faint humming sounds of approaching planes. The sounds rose gradually to the distinctive throbbing engine noises, easily identifiable as 'Jerry'. They were directly above us. Through the entrance to the shelter we could see searchlight beams cutting and criss-crossing the black fabric of night. One enemy plane was coned for several seconds before it eluded the stabbing shafts of light and the targeted anti-aircraft shells. The sky reddened with fires began by incendiaries that prepared the target for HE bombs. The crumping of these bombs became ominously louder.

Dot held me tightly as I began to shake. I am not of the stuff of which heroes are made. When later we moved to lodgings near to the city centre, we would become a little more accustomed to nightly air raids.

The Ministry of Pensions sent me a pension order book branded with a life-long personal reference number. The pension book stated that I would be paid at the rate of 32/6 (£1-62p) per week. Similar 100% disabled cases of the Great War were concurrently receiving £2 per week pension. Another anomaly: because I had married after being disabled, the union would not be recognised by the Ministry. I would not, therefore, be granted the small, related marriage allowance. The government later granted us parity with our afflicted elders and then relented generally on a ruling that might have encouraged celibacy among single war pensioners.

War pensions granted to disabled ex-service men of future wars – for example, Faulklands – would be more generous and with compensation on a scale awarded to industrial accident cases. We old, uncompensated pensioners would benefit a little from this by hanging tenaciously onto the coat tails of our younger, and better off, brethren. Unlike them, however, we would never be robbed of a financial, and fulfilling, need to work for a living.

The Ministry of Labour "requested" Dot to return to nursing, at a local hospital, leaving me again housebound. As a respite from handicraft work I started burrowing through Bill's textbooks, those of them concerned with applied mathematics. Bill himself was rarely caught at his books. He was one of those fortunate few to whom studying was an effortless task. Compared with him, I was a plodder.

One typically cheerless evening, while puffing on her post-prandial Woodbine, my mother voiced her fermented thoughts about my home-based occupation. She considered it demeaning. "You ought to have a proper job," she said. She meant, of course, one in a factory.

"I could arrange an appointment with our personnel manager," she persevered, the clamped fag wagging in her mouth threatening, but never succeeding, to jettison excess ash. "He may be able to fit you in somewhere – a sitting-down job," she said, and tried unsuccessfully to smile.

"What about travelling to work?"

"We can take it in turns to push you in the folding chair to the bus stop and then to the factory. We'll get you there somehow."

The personnel manger requested a clerk to wheel me along to a vast, ground-floor workshop where a great number of people were working with the zeal and cooperative skills of a colony of ants. Strictly geometrical layouts of machinery, lathes, millers, presses and of workbenches were cut through by straight, clear paths of grey concrete floor. The collective noises of the different machining operations, the clattering and hammering of the bench-workers, the scraping of filled workpans being dragged along the floor to waiting Lister platform trucks; the poor general lighting and the harsh localised lighting; the smell of steel being cut, shaped, pressed and welded brought it all back, submerging all other thoughts. I once had worked here milling breech blocks for machine guns, and now I was back, but with a new outlook on factory work.

It was with these mixed feelings that I shook hands with the suited workshop manager. His hands, like mine, were clean, soft and white. His would remain in that genteel condition. Beaming at me, he said he would be pleased to fix me up with a job. He introduced me to a charge-hand and two workers.

"This is Sid," he said, and a boiler-suited man rose from his stool. "Harry and Ted," the manager indicated the two seated at the long, one-sided bench who had paused in their unrelenting hammering. They briefly turned their heads in our direction. The three workers, who were all in their thirties, wore leather aprons The dark-haired charge-hand was made to look slim by the voluminous boiler suit that he wore under his. He deliberately, yet politely, declined to shake hands with me. His hands were black. The sandwich he was eating was clasped in a fold of torn newspaper. It was arranged that I joined my new workmates on Monday. Then, suitably clad and sitting on a fourth stool, I helped them to arm fighter planes.

The standard armament of the RAF's single-seat fighters was eight .303 Browning machine guns. Some Spitfires and Hurricanes were now being armed alternatively with batteries of cannon. One special version of a Hurricane, for example, sprouted four cannon firing 40 millimetre calibre armour piercing shells designed to blast the stubborn lids off German tanks.

The cannon shells were clasped in belted links. My workmates and I ensured that the individual links were finally of a precise size to house them. This we did by fitting each heavy gauge, pressed steel link onto a hefty steel mandrel, which was of identical size to a future shell, and pounding the combination on a plate anvil until they mated perfectly.

The shells, deputised by the mandrel, had to fit snugly in their links, not too loose or not too possessive a fit, that was our aim. RAF armourers, servicing planes on barren, windswept airstrips, detested links that would allow a cannon shell to wander freely. They detested even more those of them that required their charges to be driven home when loading the belts. The links, having submitted to a relentless hammering, were afterwards hinged together in belts of twenty five. That was the easiest part of the job that black-veined and calloused my once white hands but which, satisfyingly, enabled me to earn a weekly wage that was dependant upon output. With the help and support of a loving wife, I was now on the road back.

The job was not far removed from that of a smithy. It was not performed under a spreading chestnut tree, however, but under a notice, LOUSY LINKS UNLIMITED, scrawled in chalk on a ragged edged piece of cardboard hanging on the sheer brick wall facing us. Contentedly we worked alongside each other, pounding away. We shared our rationed cigarettes and our joys and woes. I sympathised with my workmates. In their 'free' time they were compelled to do either Home Guard duty or stand on the factory roof at night firewatching in case any incendiaries came their way. Gratefully I was exempted from any extensions to long working days.

As did my mother, I remained a factory worker. The one break in my long industrial life was temporary, while I was on loan to the Army. Practically, then theoretically, I would always be concerned in producing objects contrived by the fascinating art of engineering, and no better place to do that than Birmingham.

CHAPTER 17

My job had slimmed me down to bone and muscle. The loss of weight was reflected in my stumps which made it necessary for me to visit the regional artificial limb-fitting centre.

The limbfitter measured me for my second pair of limbs. To keep me active while they were being made, he lined the sockets of my existing pair. "When your new limbs are ready," the limbfitter said, "you can swop over to them. Then we'll refit the sockets of your old pair. Help him to get dressed, Fred."

Fred Rose, the young apprentice, would become, eventually, the senior limbfitter, a grandfather and a survivor of a ritual heart attack. He has kept me mobile for over fifty years with significant success. For his unstinting service to the artificial limbfitting profession he was awarded a well-earned MBE.

On leaving the limbfitting room I was waylaid by the regional manager himself, whom previously I had known only as 'your obedient servant'.

"Ah! Mr. Cottam. I noted that you were due to visit us. I should like to have a word with you. Come this way." Obediently I followed him into his vast office.

"As a double amputee well above knees you are entitled to a free issue of a hand-propelled tricycle," he said, and was just about to loll back in his swivel chair when his civil service upbringing jerked him forward. "On loan, of course."

Everything issued from the Ministry of Pensions (and its successor) to war pensioners is on loan, including our artificial limbs. Thou shalt not flog them, assuming there any buyers.

(*What the 'ell is a hand-propelled tricycle?*)

"What is a hand-propelled tricycle?"

"Tricycle? Three-wheeled thing. Small one at the front. Row it along like this." His arms made alternating saw cuts across the wide desk that separated us.

He then rummaged through a drawer and produced a linen tape measure. "I shall have to measure the lengths of your arms," he said, "the propelling levers will be adjusted to suit them."

He measured the length of each of my arms when in an out-stretched forward position. He found them to be equal in length, which did not surprise me if it did him.

I told Dot that I was to be mounted on wheels. "I shall be able to get to and from work under my own steam," I rejoiced.

"You'll be under clouds of it if you hand-propel yourself six miles to work. Then, after hammering all day and propelling yourself back home, you'll be worn out. The tricycle will be useful for getting about locally, but that's all."

The big, black-enamelled, tubular-steel tricycle had, as the manager said, a small wheel at the front and larger, bicycle-type wheels at the rear. The right hand pumping lever had a spade grip for steering the front wheel. I zoomed around locally in my new toy. As Dot had foreseen, it was tiring to propel long distances or up hills.The hired folding push-chair remained indispensable, but it was showing the signs of hard usage through taking me to and from work.

Unexpectedly an ex-service men's association came to my rescue. Since the previous war this association had had a standard arrangement with the Ministry for motorising the tricycles of war pensioners. The cost of the conversion had to be borne by an applicant. It was my personal misfortune to be thousands of lousy links short of the money.

It was then relayed to me that if the conversion was sanctioned by the Ministry, the association would bear half of the cost, which would halve the number of links needing to be hammered for this purpose. When it was sanctioned, my workmates were just as overjoyed as I was at the prospect of my becoming independently mobile.

Throughout that week Ted was quietly and mysteriously leaving the bench for long periods. I had commented to the others about Ted's absences since he himself was evasive about them. With a hint of a smile Sid kept repeating to me, "Ted's got the trots!"

We finished work earlier on Saturdays. Late Saturday afternoon I sat in my pushchair outside the factory gate and waited for whoever whose turn it was to collect me and take me home by bus. Ted came out with the last of our shift. We had already wished each other: "Good night!".

He put a grimy stuffed envelope on my lap. "We've been having a collection in the shop during the week," he explained. "That should pay for your half of the conversion."

I watched the tall, stooped figure in the shabby mac as he walked homeward. He looked back and, with a triumphant grin, waved to me.

Thus began a seven-year apprenticeship to a converted trike, a motorised invalid carriage, my 'chariot,' as I dubbed it. A two-stroke engine, mated to a two-speed gearbox, was slung between the replacement motor cycle wheels at the rear end of the chariot. Chromium plated hand controls sprouted from the sides of the cockpit. Headlamp and rear lamp had been shrouded to restrict emitted light to mere slits to conform with the strict blackout regulations. The converter's wavering confidence in the reliability of the engine was revealed by the retention of the hand-propelling gear. The engine ran on one part oil to sixteen parts petrol – thoroughly pre-mixed. I carried a mixing can on board to ensure that it was.

The total weight of my chariot was over three hundredweight (if you prefer, 155 kilogrammes). The added weight of a driver, even a lightweight one, made it imperative that the overstressed, single cylinder engine was well maintained.

Stability at speed was not one of my chariot's stronger points. Normal maximum speed, cross winds permitting, was about 30 mph, which went modestly unrecorded through the absence of a speedometer. Once travelled a timed nineteen miles (between signposts) on the A1 in exactly thirty minutes and the overheated engine had threatened to boil the petrol mixture stored in the tank positioned just above it.

Later models sheltered their drivers from the elements and were fitted with engines of adequate power. This earlier, open model that I drove for seven years had been unchanged in its basic design since it was evolved just after the Great War. It was the original Grand Prix Bathchair.

My chariot transformed my life. In spite of its shortcomings it enabled me to get around unescorted, providing I had sufficient rationed petrol coupons. However, I was a lonely traveller. Joint outings were made separately with Dot making a parallel journey, without the company of a burden-sharing husband, on a bus or train.

Relationships with other members of the family in our council house home were now becoming strained. Personal opinions were being suppressed. Irritations were mounting up. Nicotine failed to soothe and, indeed, acted as a catalyst.

Without exception, all the family smoked cigarettes. Whoever among us brought home a ration of cigarettes put them in the sideboard drawer and was reimbursed by Mam. Anyone who extracted a packet was trusted to leave the price of it in the 'till', the nominal cutlery tray that slid along the top of the drawer and which shut off a faint fragrance of tobacco. This trading system relied entirely on the numeracy and honesty of all its members. It was noticed that the system was not running smoothly even though we all could add up.

Mam had been delayed leaving for work through trying to equate the coins in the till with the absent cigarettes. "There is not enough money here to cover the cost of the cigarettes taken out," Mam said obliquely addressing the opened drawer. She tried to sound surprised but her tone was false.

Bill, pausing in his preparations for a night shift, curled his lip. That economical expression eloquently conveyed his opinion of transactions based foolishly on trust.

I had quickly detected that money in the tray rarely tallied with packets that once had been stored underneath it. To avoid further friction in the household I had kept quiet about the disparities.

The individual prices of packets of Woodbines, Park Drive, Players and the scarce Senior Service were standardised. The prices of oddly named cigarettes that were introduced to the aromatic drawer, varied in accordance with their source of supply. Packets of these brands were much more vulnerable to instant discounting when extracted.

Shortages and rationing had been responsible for the spawning of these strange brands of cigarettes that normally would have found not too ready a market. One brand, with its cigarettes made from a compound of Turkish and other exotic tobaccoes, was named Pasha. Only Mam, when desperate could smoke them. This led to her having 'Pasha' prefixed to her Christian name.

Pasha Nell turned her gaze from the drawer and viewed us all through disillusioned eyes. In the tensioning moments Bill slowly buttoned up his faithful overcoat, looped its belt and, with another contemptuous curl of his lip, departed for work.

"I've paid for my fags!" Dai trumpeted to emphasise his innocence and to remove himself from the rank of suspects. Which left Dot and me.

Pasha picked up her things and left for work without saying another word. Dai retreated to his bedroom. Pat, the lodger, who had sensed an impending family quarrel, tactfully had gone out immediately after the late main meal. In the descending silence, Dot and I gazed at each other sorrowfully.

"We shall have to leave this unhappy house," Dot said.

We were fortunate to find a vacant bed-sitting room. The move would bring us into the central target zone for enemy bombers, but the risks had to be accepted.

The house with the room to let was terraced, old and decrepit. The front gardens of the row of crumbling villas extended a mere two metres to the long and low boundary wall that defined the width of the pavement. The wall was abruptly pillared at the entrances to identical front doors. Pairs of hinge hooks were still embedded in the pillars. Wrought iron gates once hung on them and had been surrendered in a war-time scrap-metal collecting drive.

It was a much busier neighbourhood than the one we intended leaving. There were shops and clanking, rumbling electric tramcars swayed downhill sparking their way to Saltley Gate, the drivers twiddling their big brass handles and clanging on foot bells. The blank expressions of the shoppers may have concealed waning hopes of the war ending victoriously. We were now in the darkest, dreariest period of the war.

Our proposed landlady's two children, young boys, seemed uncontrollable. When their blowsy, ginger-haired mother invited us inside to show us the vacant front room, the boys were bringing up coal from the cellar. An unseen offspring was down the dark hole hurling lumps of coal to his brother at the top of the steps who was catching most of them, noisily, in a galvanised bucket.

"If you two don't do that quietly, I'll bang your bleedin' 'eads together!" she screamed down the hall.

"I'll show you the room," she said with a switched-on sweetness. We agreed a rent along with certain facilities and it became our first home.

On my return home from work at night, Dot and I manhandled the silenced chariot onto the brick-paved path leading to the front door and then swung it under the bay window of our room. An improvised cover gave it an added protection from the worst of the wintry weather.

There was no protection at all from the prevailing bitterly cold weather for neither chariot nor driver when bonded in flight. I drove to work on those dark mornings with head bowed and shoulders braced against piercing winds, interspersed with freezing rain. As I was not yet re-hardened to severely cold weather, I succumbed to pneumonia.

The instant I ceased working I ceased earning. Providently, Dot had been found a job at a local confectioners and her small wage paid the rent. As she was working locally Dot was able to double as nurse.

After I had been confined to bed for several weeks, the doctor allowed me to get up for a few hours daily. "But you must not go outdoors," he warned.

I couldn't. Firstly, I had gradually to accustom myself again to wearing coupled artificial limbs before attempting to stagger outside and escape from the claustrophobic sick room.

Hideous flower-patterned wallpaper, which we had inherited, vied for contempt with our landlady's jarring black and white copies of the 'Crossing Sweeper' and Landseer's 'Stag at Bay' that hung above the fireplace. Early evenings red coals from the kitchen fire were placed in our grate to quickly start another. The subdued lighting and the dancing shadows of the flickering flames then helped to keep the vulgar decor, as well as the stag, at bay.

Though physically weakened by my illness, I gladly returned to my job. The illness was also mentally lowering and could possibly have triggered a delayed nervous reaction to my war injuries. I became depressed, disorientated and wracked with self doubt. The young, black physician, who had been very kind and attentive to me, now turned psychiatrist.

"Go out and have pint now and then," he said. So, I did as he suggested – in fact, still do. But it was Dot who was mainly responsible for picking me up psychologically. It was Dot who provided stability.

A difficult decision had to be made if I wanted to raise myself to the status of a professional engineer. It would be a long haul to obtain the necessary academic qualifications, but I could not study and work long hours in a factory.

Supported by a medical note from my accommodating black doctor, I applied to be released from my job. Compassionately, the company doctor signed the Ministry of Labour form that permitted me to finish working at the munitions' factory.

CHAPTER 18

"This is the mitre jig with the various lengths marked on it. Tenon saw, pin hammer, panel pins, beading. I'll bring you a further supply of beading when I call to collect the finished picture frames. Let me show you how to make one."

The shrunken little man placed a jig on the board that temporarily covered the gas stove. He put a lath beaded with black and gilt moulding into the jig and, using the saw, produced the paired sides of a picture frame.

"Use this guide to pin the sides together," he said and tapped the pins home. A completed frame was ready to receive glass and picture.

The spiv-like character never divulged the precise destination of the great numbers of garish picture frames I became adept at making, whether they were for a legitimate or black market. I was paid a pittance for my work but was thankful to be earning even that little amount to add to my small pension while studying at home.

We were living in a one-bedroomed, ground floor, council maisonette. That helpful ex-service association had prodded the City Housing Department to provide us with it.

The living room was partly furnished with a 'Utility' manufactured dining suite, acquired with a buying permit. The simulated oak was not of a poor quality for it was made to a wartime specification. The plywood backing of the sideboard, however, revealed its lowly origins: the sides of a packing case. A stencilled monogram stated boldly, 'Tate & Lyle'. Until we could afford two easy chairs we had to sit upright at the table as if perpetually dining, but it did not dent our pride in our first real home.

We were more in touch with Pasha now that we were living nearby. Bill, having been accepted by the RAF, had been trained as the navigator of a Mosquito. Dai had enlisted in the 6th. Airborne Division and was stationed in Northern Ireland. Tony was still in Canada so Pasha had none of her sons living at home. She was still working on night shifts at the factory where I had worked days. Pat, the lodger, remained in the quietened home, alternating his working hours with those of Pasha's.

The Education Department wanted to see me about my application for a grant to enable me to enter a university. The optimistic charioteer drove to the city centre to meet his intending sponsors. A weak, spring sun struggled, and failed, to match his uplifted spirits.

My interviewer was urbane, confident and slightly too suave. In a soft, upper-class voice he quietly dashed my hopes of entering a university and condemned me to a further spell of picture-frame making.

With barely suppressed pride he began: "A university degree is a great asset in a chosen career." He extended a fake smile and allowed me moment to dwell on his own personal achievement while he set me up for a big drop. "And we," he continued, "are empowered to assist persons, such as yourself who, on returning to civilian life, wish to go to university."

Then, his voice descended a few semitones. "However, grants are available only to those applicants whose formal education was suspended by the present – emergency. In your case, no academic studies were interrupted since none were being undertaken," he said with a faint suggestion of acid courtliness.

"Now, if you held a Higher School Certificate, or if you had have matriculated, we would be in a position to help you because either of these qualifications would make you acceptable for entrance to a university," he explained.

On noticing my dejected look he smoothed his sparse greying

hair and appeared to consult his conscience. Rallying, he said in a gentle sotto voice: "I would advise you to undertake an engineering course at a technical college."

He seemed mildly disdainful of technical colleges. Nonetheless it proved sound advice.

Chastened, I drove round to the Central Technical College. Appropriately, it was raining, steadily, and the greyness of the day now matched my mood. The college had extended its teaching hours to include Saturdays to help working students with limited spare time. Paying the small annual fee I enrolled on a Saturday engineering course, leaving myself available for a job during the week.

Concurrently, I planned to study to matriculate. Pasha's French grammars, though old and with quaint Tenniel-style illustrations, should be of help with my obligatory second language subject.

"How did you get on?" Dot asked me.

"So so. Not eligible for a university grant because I didn't go to a grammar school. I've signed up for a technical college course – Saturdays."

"Well, that's a start. You can't really study engineering subjects at home. You need tuition," Dot said, giving me an encouraging smile as she resumed ironing. "By the way, *he's* been. He's taken the frames and left a few shillings."

Next day, on my return from the local library with some borrowed text books, Dot told me that the personnel manager of an automobile accessories manufacturer, to whom I had written, would like to see me. "You might be offered a job." Her face was alight with happiness. She had already brushed and pressed my wedding suit.

The seven miles ride in my chariot thawed my frozen aspirations. It had taken thirty minutes to get into the central industrial area of the city. I had timed the journey hoping that it would be done regularly.

"We are prepared to train you as a product designer," the efficient personnel manager said. "We are also prepared to grant you one full day release from work every week for a few years to allow you to continue with your studies at the Central Technical College. That will save you having to go there on Saturdays. In any case, you'll be working here Saturday mornings. Regarding pay, you will be put on a clerical scale until we see how you progress. Report to the Ignition Section Leader in the Production Drawing Office – I'll ring to tell him that you are on your way. Turn left when you leave here – left again at the corner – then ask for the PDO. Hope you do well, Mr. Cottam," he said as we shook hands.

If able, I would have jumped for joy on staggering out into the street! The job with it's weekly pay packet meant the end of my scraping a living making picture frames.

The afternoon sun was shining brightly but did not reach down to the shaded streets that separated the mammoth factory blocks. The enclosed darkened spaces of the complex resonated with the low, continuous humming of unseen machinery.

I parked my chariot in the tunnel-like entrance of the located block. Anticipating a gap in the contra-flowing Lister trucks, laden and unladen, I walked over to a brightly polished, Great War ribboned commissionaire to ask further directions. He spotted my disabled ex-service man's lapel badge and his officious attitude visibly softened. To save me climbing five flights of stairs he led me to a goods lift.

"'The Penthouse'," he let slip to the lift attendant.

The massive, open-plan office was bisected by a main thoroughfare. On one side of this aisle was a forest of easelled drawing boards in parallel rows. Each double row of boards, headed by a segregated little office off the aisle, constituted a complete design section. Ignition Section was jammed between Lamps and Switchgear.

Mr. Smith, the section leader was in his late forties. Outwardly he was a greyish man – grey hair, pale grey face with steel grey eyes, dark grey suit. But there was nothing colourless about his personality. He was brash and chillingly ambitious.

"Sir down, Bo," he requested when I had introduced myself. He called everyone, except his superiors, "Bo". Apparently the habit stemmed from his period in America working as a production engineer.

"So you want to be a product designer?" Bo Smith said when I had sat down uncomfortably close to him in the cramped little office.

I said: "Yes..."

His phone rang. Swift instructions were issued to someone who would have barely time to take them in.

"We don't usually offer to train someone who has not served an apprenticeship in a toolroom," he said," but you have industrial experience and we are short staffed. Though work here is classed as a reserved occupation, staff have volunteered for the Forces," he explained with a wry half smile.

His phone jumped again.

He breathed out. "Starting from scratch you will have a lot to learn, here as well as at tech. Briefly, production engineering is mainly about efficiency, accuracy and a disciplined approach to the job in hand. A dimensional mistake on a drawing could result in thousands of those parts being mass produced before the fault is discovered. All information on a drawing therefore has to be checked, then double checked. Some design offices employ experienced 'checkers'. We don't. Every designer here is personally responsible for his own work. My signature appended to a drawing is the only nominal one."

His shoulder brushed mine as again he picked up an invasive instrument. The section leader half rose from his chair and called out a name. A white-haired man with creased features lodged a pencil behind an ear and took the proffered phone.

"Well, Bo, you'll be starting on Monday. This will be your board." It was the first one in a line and next to his office. "See you then." We did not waste his valuable time by shaking hands.

Dot was elated when I told her the good news. We promised ourselves a night out at the Hippodrome when I received my first week's pay.

"I don't suppose you have any drawing instruments?" Bo Smith asked me on my first morning at work. "I'll ask 'Promising Joe' to get you a second-hand set. We'll have to keep reminding him. He's the floor manager and the only one here who can get these things.

In the meantime, the others in the section will help you out with their spares and with log tables," he said generously.

"I'm going to put you under a senior designer for a while. You will detail parts from his layouts. Two pencils, 3H and 4H. Because of the war we are short of them so you will have to produce a stub to get it replaced with a new one. Here's an extension sleeve to help you to use the last bit of pencil."

Right on cue, his phone rang. "Ask around if you need anything," he said as he sidestepped back into his office.

I was amazed at the amount of paper work required for an accessory unit. Each component part had its individual drawing, an image of threatening thousands.

The self-assertive Bo Smith told me: "We find it laughable when we read about the design of a secret submarine being drawn on the back of an old envelope. The many drawings of something that size and complexity would fill this entire office!"

It was a little unsettling at first working in a clean office, where everyone wore their best clothes, and where the ramparts of class distinction were still being manned by some of the office staff, notably by clerks who felt much superior to manual workers. Technical staff, having graduated from workshops, did not adopt such a snobbish attitude towards a former training ground.

A clerk in the big office, who dressed faultlessly in country tweeds, used to spread his financial newspaper on his desk at dinner time – sorry, lunch break. One day, as I passed by, he looked up from columns of figures to ask me if I had any 'rubbah'.

"Rubber what?" I enquired naively, and added to his fears about the infiltrating masses.

The gradual shift to the left in politics during the latter part of the war was beginning to get to him. His technical associates, trade union members, rubbed it in by addressing each other loudly as comrade and, in mock formality, citizen. It would be easier for me to adjust to working in an office than it would be for him to adapt to living in a politically changing environment.

The technical college showed up my physical limitations more than it did my mental ones. As there were no handrails to the cascading front steps of the technical college they were an obstacle that I never surmounted without help so I parked my chariot at the rear of the building and used the 'trademen's' entrance. There were still a few disappointing steps for me to climb and again no handrail. One wall however was clad with grimy service pipes, the exposed innards of the building. I carried an old glove to grip the coolest of my improvised handrails.

The old college was a tall building with many floors. Laboratories using heavy testing and experimental equipment had staked claim to the lower floors. The complementary lectures were delivered in rooms in the upper regions of the building.

A key to the lift was issued officially to me along with the warning that, in view of the war-time shortage of maintenance staff, I might not be able to use it very often. On finding that the lift rarely responded to a signal I returned the token key to the registrar's office.

Fortunately, the spiralling wide mosaic steps to the elevated floors were balustraded. Students and lecturers, known and unknown to me, helpfully carried my bulged brief case and one of my sticks as I hauled myself upwards. This camaraderie reminded me of my Army days.

The lecture rooms, heavy with varnished wood, were like amphitheatres. Typically, the students' entrance doorway led onto the topmost row of wooden benches, which rose steeply in concentric curves from the lecturer's lone desk. The high desk was framed by a big, very wide blackboard. The lecturer came on stage through a personal door alongside it.

The tiers of benches were in blocks to allow the steps to tumble down freely between them. I had always to sit in the topmost row, near to our entrance door. An attempt at even one step downward, to be nearer the rest of a class, would have invited a trip in an ambulance. To give me personal tuition the lecturers were always prepared to climb up to the solitary figure sitting quietly by himself in the back row of a lecture room.

In the next decade the old technical college would be raised in status, first to a college of advanced technology and finally to a technological university. Throughout these academically historic times a mature student sat 'oniztod' in the gods, latterly on dark evenings, and recalls doing so with pleasure and gratitude. He didn't go to a university – it came to him.

Dot's pregnancy was confirmed. The thought of becoming a father made me feel even more grateful for my job.

Ma arrived from Yorkshire to take charge of her daughter and the expected baby while I was at work. No sooner was a helpful mother-in-law installed when Dot developed toxemia and had to be rushed into the city maternity hospital. Veronica was born the following week. She looked exactly like all the other babies in the ward with surgical-tape labels on their tiny wrists, except she had more hair than the others.

I was fortunate to be allowed inside the maternity hospital to see my wife and daughter. There was a prevailing flu epidemic and all visiting had been banned temporarily. The matron, to whom I had grovelled for admittance to the ward, had relented when faced with the beseeching, doleful look that I reserve for such emergencies. She was rewarded with my cheerful transformation.

A policeman, waiting alone outside the hospital for me to return from the ward one very cold early evening, was not quite so obliging.

"This your vehicle!" he demanded rather than asked. Since I was on two sticks and the solitary parked vehicle in the road was an invalid carriage, I was tempted to congratulate him on his brilliant impersonation of Sherlock Holmes. Sensibly, I resisted the impulse.

"Yes - why...?"

"No lights!"

"Not unless the engine is running," I tried to explain. (Very little light emitted then because of the masking.)

"Well, if it has no parking lights, leave it on the pavement so that other road users can proceed safely in the blackout."

"Yes, constable."

The next night a police sergeant told me to park the chariot in the road and not on the pavement where it was a dangerous obstruction to pedestrians in the blackout.

"Yes, sergeant."

Ma was delighted to see her first grandchild. As soon as I could manage at home unaided, Ma returned to her own home, to four other helpless males, Dad and his dad, young Tom and George, the family lodger.

Veronica was two weeks old on Christmas Day and she was already showing, or I was first noticing, the unique characteristics of an individual baby. Naturally, I hoped that she would retain the cornflower blue colour of her eyes.

We were issued with a special gas mask for our child. It was a totally enclosing box-like contraption. We hoped that we would never have to fit the baby into the frightening thing.

My chariot was now jibbing at the regular journeys to work and tech. and the occasional long trips to Yorkshire and Lancashire. It was cruelly exposed to the rigours of the weather and a lot of my time was taken up in keeping it roadworthy.

We applied to the Housing Department for an exchange maisonette much nearer to my work to reduce my daily mileage. Finally, we were offered one in a two-storey block in Hockley. It was left to Dot to look over our proposed new home.

"It's an end, ground floor maisonette. If necessary, you could just about manage to walk from it to the office," Dot reported. "There are two bedrooms, a living room and a small kitchen." It sounded marvellous.

"But..." Dot paused and struggled to recapture her initial enthusiasm, "it is in a filthy condition! I told the clerk so when I returned the keys. He said he would arrange for the maisonette to be thoroughly cleaned."

When I saw the place it was obvious that an attempt had been made to make a hovel appear presentable. Only wallpaper, when obtainable, would completely obliterate the crudely drawn 'squander bugs' on the walls.

We were standing in the middle of the bare living room when Dot raised her eyes heavenwards. I knew what she was thinking: whom would we have above us this time?

The children of our present overhead neighbour had broken into our home one night while we were at the local cinema. It was a frightening experience returning to a fouled home, not knowing if the intruders, whoever they were, had been disturbed or had left. They had left, I discovered, and put down the poker.

Nothing had been stolen. We had hardly anything of monetary value, anyway. We fell out with the children's parents over the break-in because we had immediately reported it to the police. We were unaware that it was a tribal matter that could have been settled with head bangings.

Our new vertical neighbours were a young couple with two children. The husband was a habitual thief who was now on parole from prison. He turned out to be a friendly bloke who, though still making the weight, did not practise his art locally.

The local shops were not far away. There was a small church just up the little hill. The church was built long before the Victorian terraced houses that now surrounded it. There was a pub on the way to church, or on the way back. Opposite the pub crouched an accommodating pawnshop. Two more pubs beckoned at the other end of the street. These three inns catered for the devout of both sects. The two in the same direction belonged to Ansells Brewery. 'The Swan', opposite the pawnshop, represented the opposition, Mitchells & Butlers.

We moved in on the fourth day of the fourth month 1944. It was a dull day with an overcast sky and Mrs. Nelson called to greet us.

I opened the door at the end of a thin hall onto a woman of about my mother's age. Mrs. Nelson was short, rotund, and she had fringed black hair, streaked grey. She also had a well-defined moustache. Dressed plainly, she wore a spotlessly clean apron, her emblem, it transpired, for she was never seen without one.

Standing pigeon-toed in the doorway she wheezed breathlessly, "I'm Mrs. Nelson. I live in a maisonette round the corner."

"Dot and Eric Cottam," I responded "won't you come in?"

"No, not today, thank you. You carry on with your unpacking. Thought I'd just call to see if you needed any help. If you find that you do, don't be afraid to ask."

Turning her head in the direction of the outside world she said, "You'll find everyone round here easy to get along with. Most of the younger men are away – in the Forces. You've been in the Army," she said glancing down at the two sticks I was clasping in one hand to confirm what she obviously had heard from that mine of housing information, the rent collector.

Oddly, Mrs. Nelson's head did not return to a normal, central position when swung back on its pivot. It remained slightly off-centre as if she was half looking over her shoulder. Aware that I was looking at her curiously she broke out: "The brook is quiet today."

"Brook? Quiet?"

"Hockley Brook, behind that wall," she said indicating the high wall that ran parallel with the end of our block. A brook would explain the reason for an unusually wide gap between two blocks of maisonettes.

"In wet weather it rises and roars as it rushes under the street. Not long ago, after a storm, the brook flooded the district. We had to claim for our damaged or lost possessions. Nearly every household had lost gold watches!" Her eyes were slits of mirth.

Composing her round face she said, "It does pong at times. When it does, you get on to the Health Department."

As the neighbourly and permanently aproned Mrs. Nelson waddled back home it struck me why she had turned her head a little peculiarly to one side when viewing closely. Having met similarly afflicted war pensioners I should have known the reason. Mrs. Nelson, like her illustrious namesake, had only one available eye. The other one looked but it did not see.

Prolonged wet weather did cause the brook to rise and to roar at being throttled at the restricting entrance of the culvert that ran under the street. The Niagara-like roaring seemed as if in protest at having, after only a few hundred yards of heavenly daylight, to be forced under the earth to recommence its Stygian meanderings. It was maintained by some of the locals that the subterranean course of Hockley Brook was not completely charted, there being no accurate records after the city had been dumped over it. During its

197

charted or uncharted course it associated with unsavoury company. When it finally emerged for that short stretch in Hockley it vented spasmodically a truly awful stench that, contrarily, was more offensive in cooler weather.

A milk bottling company upstream was accused regularly by us, the disenchanted brookside residents, of purposely allowing their waste products to seep into the brook. The company spokesman, just as regularly, was predictably outraged at the unfounded accusations of the local peasantry.

Representing the neighbourhood I formally complained to the Health Department about an environmental unpleasantness. A remote Department representative, who loftily replied to my letter, said that odours from the brook were extremely rare and were not injurious to health. So, when the dun-coloured brook turned whitish and stank to high heaven, the brookside residents would officially remain healthy.

CHAPTER 19

The Dental Hospital, another academy of learning, was not far from the technical college. It offered free dental treatment (unique in those days) to those prepared to run a gauntlet of probing inspections. In an attempt to overcome my fear of dentists, rooted in me since my orphanage days, I attended the training hospital for regular check-ups.

Routine x-rays taken on my last visit revealed that I had impacted wisdom teeth. When the news was relayed to me I thought, in my ignorance, that it was something of an achievement, proving that wisdom does not always arrive with these latecomers.

"Waggle your jaws like this," a dental surgeon requested, sliding his jaws to and fro. His junior emphasised my anticipated jaw movements by bouncing his chin off the opposite walls. Ever obedient, I did as told.

"That's when you find it painful!" DS pronounced in an implied congratulatory tone.

"...you find it painful," his assistant repeated, lagging respectfully.

"Not really," I confessed warily.

"Remarkable!" the junior exclaimed giving his senior a prompting glance.

"Nevertheless, if we leave them there, they will turn nasty," DS said smiling thinly. "We shall have to get you admitted to the Queen Elizabeth Hospital for a general operation to have them extracted."

That put the wind up me vertically. The Dental Hospital preferred to send me to the QE for a dental operation! Obviously, it must be serious.

I was in there a week.

When I came round after the op it felt as if my jaws had been patted with a sledge hammer. It was painful even to think about opening my mouth. My face was swollen, bruised and a patchy-blue colour. Tyre levers must have been used to keep my mouth open during the operation. When opened beyond even its greatest extent the surgeon must have had his elbows inside my mouth to affect his excavations. Surgery completed, my jaws had been snapped shut, and had then latched.

Two wordless days later the surgeon's young assistant came to my bedside and caught me unawares.

"I'm going to remove the packing from the cavities," he said brightly looking down at his wild-eyed, mute patient. Prising apart my clamped jaws with his enormous grip he fished for long and narrow lengths of gauze with his tweezers. The pillow case absorbed more blood.

"You'll have some debri work out of the cavities," he said grinning and exposing an array of perfect teeth. "Nothing to worry about."

Dot and Veronica came to collect me from the hospital on 8 May 1945. As we were leaving the antiseptic smells behind us a hurrying doctor, stethoscope wildly swinging around his neck, flung back the remark that Veronica was 'a bonny child.'

We returned home on an inner circle bus. The driver, having recognised us, considerately 'moved' the bus stop and dropped us off at our maisonette to save me a short walk.

That afternoon bonfires were laid, to be lit later, in the street of maisonette blocks, squashed terrace houses and a button factory. Meanwhile, before the tarmac was warmed up, children were going to have a party on the trestle tables erected along the centre of the street. Veronica became very excited at the prospect of a children's party.

Of course, it was VE Day! A week in hospital, and a massive

face ache to show for it, had driven most things out of my mind.

'The Swan', on the corner, though a beer house and not a public house and therefore restricted to the sale of beer only, was shut normally at this time of day. It was now doing a roaring trade. I was immediately found a seat. Wafer-thin sandwiches were specially prepared for me by the kindly landlady. Forcing open a reluctant mouth to a mere slit, I slid them in. The 'gottle a geer' I requested ventriloquially was drunk through a straw.

A 'greasy pole' bridged the street. Mrs. Nelson, perched precariously above our heads, slithered successfully from one side of the street to the other, her active orb gleaming. Everyone else who accepted the challenge fell untidily onto nervously waiting helpers below.

The plonking piano that effectively closed off one end of the street kept reminding us that we were going to hang up our washing on the Siegfried Line. Spontaneous, frenetic dancing around the piano continued throughout the night until the pub shut in the early morning – so I was told. Steered by a caring wife I had staggered home on discovering that people with hollow legs cannot drink more than those with solid ones. Not through a straw, anyway. When the bed came round to me, I fell onto it.

It was an unforgettable day that had been celebrated with a fervour of relief that the war in Europe was finally over. VJ Day came as an anti-climax and was not quite so boisterously celebrated in the streets of Hockley, but more holes were burnt in the tarmac.

Just after the first celebration, young men in ill-fitting 'demob' suits began to trickle home. Lonely wives now became paired, sometimes oddly, with husbands and the district became less of a female place. There were gaps in some families, however, that sadly never would be filled. When grief eased and gently edged towards pride, creased sepia photographs, taken out of toffee tin boxes, were mounted in new frames.

Apart from journeys to tech., I did not depend entirely on my chariot for getting about the city. We were living on the clockwise and anti clockwise inner circle bus route. Office colleagues could view our breakfast table as their double-decker buses decelerated when passing either way to the opposite stops near to our home. A little lack of privacy, however, was a small price to pay for the convenience of a reliable bus service.

Longer journeys were always by chariot even though once helpful signposts were mostly pointing in random directions from within council depots: councils were in no hurry to re-erect signposts because there was still little traffic on the roads. The alternative, travelling by either rail or coach, created more problems for the severely disabled than were solved. Though the major railway companies allowed a user of an invalid tricycle free travel on their lines, both tricycle and user had to remain in the guard's van. I took advantage of this concession on just three occasions. The first time I did so was when visiting Dot's home as her new husband. I returned by road. The second was a trip from our home to Leatherhead, Surrey, and I returned by road. The third was Cleethorpes to Pontefract and that finished it.

The guard's vans were misnamed for they were unguarded. A lone concessionary was locked in a box with his trike and effectively cut off from the outside world. No light, no heat, no communication, no lavatory and nothing to drink. Just goods to stare at throughout a long, rumbling journey. To Yorkshire it was tightly crated, squawking, feather shedding chickens. To Leatherhead, it was something in a draped long box that was obviously on a non-return ticket to a final destination. To Pontefract it was boxes of fish. Thereafter I travelled solo on long, pioneering journeys while my wife and daughter made parallel trips on coaches or trains.

One long trip, to begin a summer holiday at my parents- in-law's home, exposed the limitations of both chariot and driver. Foolishly I had allowed that sunny day to beguile me into travelling a different route to Yorkshire. Instead of driving again through bland Nottinghamshire, I would attempt a scenic route through the Peak District. If I had closely examined the sinister little numbers enclosed within wavy lines on my map, I would have realised that the Peak District is aptly named. There's one born every minute.

It was in Leek, apparently, where I stopped in a little quiet square to ask a man for directions to Buxton. Slowly, ever so slowly, he released the bent cigarette that had been pasted to his lower lip and stabbed it at the chariot. "In that!" he said incredulously.

"I've driven from Birmingham in it," I replied defensively.

"Not up the kind of hills you'll meet on the way to Buxton," he prophesied.

My hurt expression must have made it clear that I would prefer him to adopt a more helpful attitude. "First right and carry straight on," he said with a discouraging grin.

I put-putted along a nameless road, past rising fields partitioned with casual geometry by dry-stone walls. Then the road went suddenly vertical. My confidence in my trusty chariot soared after ascending this steep hill, and then plummeted when it failed to reach the summit of another one.

As I was resting the overheated engine, I was spotted by soldiers out on manoeuvres and they kindly pushed me up to the

top of the hill. After failing to reach the top of the next one, which had merged with the rarefied atmosphere, I decided to attack it slyly in a series of loops – free-wheel downhill, let in the clutch and charge back up hoping to pass the starting point before the engine shuddered to a depressingly familiar stop. It worked on Loop One, and better still on Two, and the summit enticingly came nearer.

Then the suppressed power of centrifugal force asserted itself on Loop Three. It snatched me from the cockpit and threw me into the ditch when over-confidently I had turned sharply in the road to charge back up the hill. The disunited chariot, relieved of its top-heavy burden rocked itself steady and accelerated up the hill on the set throttle, as it had been taught. Helpless, egg-eyed and with a grim fascination, I watched my faithless chariot desert me. If it shot over the top of the hill, and there seemed nothing to prevent it from doing so, I would be left stranded.

Fortunately, the chariot tended to steer to the left because the engine lopsidedly drove the off-side wheel. The driverless chariot veered to the left, towards the verge. It then ran along the verge and tipped over into the ditch. The engine raced madly and the upended driven wheel spun furiously, futilely. There was a likelihood of escaping fuel making a bonfire of the penitent chariot.

Spurred on by the screaming engine, I shuffled backwards up the ditch, which luckily was dry, and dragged myself along to the overturned chariot. I switched off the fuel supply, pulled back the jammed throttle lever and cut the engine. Somehow I managed to heave the heavy chariot to an upright position. Amply provided with fallen masonry from crumbling dry-stone walls, I jammed lichened stones under both rear wheels. Gathering my jettisoned belongings, walking sticks, fuel mixing can and lunch box, I assembled them nearby and, using the chariot as a support, I hauled myself back on board – gingerly. One slip and we both would be back in the ditch with me under a weighty vehicle.

After reloading the footwell with my belongings, I lay back exhausted, thankful to be reunited with my faithful chariot. I was unhurt but my clothes had suffered, particularly my light raincoat.

It had tried gallantly to restrain its wearer when he was in unrestrainable flight and a pocket, which had caught on a lever, was badly torn.

While resting I ate my packed sandwiches and reflected on the folly of attempting, what proved to be, the lonely, high altitude route to Yorkshire. Stray black-faced sheep on the verge paused in their monotonous munching to observe me with interest. Others, better positioned in the gallery, gazed over a crumbling wall at me as if wondering what will he do next? I reversed an opinion of these close croppers of grass and their uninvited companion. After all, the sheep had to be here, the intruder was the real mutton head.

To "reduce" the lowest gear I rode the clutch threatening to burn it out as I crawled up the last part of the hill. Surely, it must now be downhill to Buxton?

My dishevelled appearance drew comments when eventually I drove into the back yard of my in-law's home. On noticing Dot's anxious expression I glossed over the events of the day that had caused me to arrive much later than expected.

Ma greeted me affectionately. "Doing well with your studying, Dot tells me."

Veronica, her chubby arms outstretched, toddled across the yard to greet me. She pushed me against the wall. I propped my sticks against the large zinc bath hanging there and lifted her up, marvelling at her radiantly happy face and bright chestnut hair.

We sat on plain wooden chairs round the scrubbed kitchen table for our evening meal. Dad was the first to rise, scraping his chair harshly on the grey flagstone floor. The amber piece on the gold watch chain looped across his dull-coloured waistcoat dangled and fell into place. The stone had helped many children cut their milk teeth. Dad picked up his cap, which he had been sitting in.

That old flat cap, its original colours long become an indeterminate faded brown, was constantly with him. He had steadfastly refused to donate it to a rug being pegged, a hearth rug with a colourful diamond taking shape at its centre.

To nobody, and yet to everybody, Dad said: "Aye." To me he said, with impressive gravity, "See you down at t'Club."

Unhurriedly he left the room and the sound was heard of the back door latch being lifted.

I looked forward to a game of dominoes and a couple of beers with my amiable father-in-law and his cronies in the old Working Men's Club. It would be a consoling end to a trying day.

Dad was treasurer of his club. Conscious of his immense responsibilities, he was always among the last to leave the premises at night. Gravely drunk, he would nightly plod his way home along the unadopted road, over protruding stones that shook his bent, aged frame. Next morning he would be just as gravely sober. He worried about nowt.

I was often to cross the Pennines in my chariot, but never again would I attempt to drive it along the back of the mountain chain, and would not have done so even if I had been offered a big brass clock. Future trips to and from Yorkshire in my underpowered chariot were made through bland, hospitable Nottinghamshire.

That weekend, in gratitude to my chariot for delivering me safely home, I decided to 'decoke' its engine. Discarding my cumbersome artificial limbs to give me more freedom to work, I sat on the paving slabs outside our front door and dismantled the engine. As I was carefully remounting the piston the right way round on the piston rod a shadow loomed over me.

I looked up, and hardly recognised him. His face showed signs of more batterings in the ring and he was now built like a pocket battleship.

He knelt and embraced me. I was powerless and could not defend myself. His eyes were shining and there was a dazzling smile on his sun-tanned face.

"I was told where to find you," Len cried, "and that you had married. How are you, me old mate!"

EPILOGUE

The book has already had its proper ending and there was no intention of adding to it, but now I feel that it should be rounded off with a few words about the reactions of physically disabled people and the reactions of able-bodied to them.

According to one medical authority, disabled people can be divided – too neatly, perhaps – into three groups:

a) Those with an exaggerated determination to overcome the disability; the posture is machistic, aggressive. They are driven to attempt what they never might have previously attempted, such as climbing mountains. Instead of being part of society they prefer to remain aloof from it, yet, contrarily, wish to draw attention to themselves.

b) Those with a defeatist attitude with a tendency to depression: a sad group whose members merit sympathy but to withhold it might be more helpful.

c) Those blessed with a stable, well-balanced personality who have endeavoured to avoid the paths trodden by the above two extremes.

If I have to be classified, I shall elect myself to group 'c' for I have neither the ability nor the urge to scale mountains and this physical limitation and surmised flaw in my character does not depress me.

Similarly, able-bodied people, when confronted by someone who is greatly physically handicapped, can also be divided into three groups:

a) Those who are simply appalled.

b) Those who are coldly indifferent.

c) Those who are sympathetic and considerate, if at first torn between fright and compassion.

If any in the first two groups of these observers would go so far as to condone the practice of an African tribe to kill a severely maimed member, I should like to be removed from their mailing list. Those in these two minority groups are unlikely to change their attitudes. Let us concern ourselves therefore with the reactions to us of the last group, where, thankfully, most able-bodied people dwell.

The sight of someone wearing a wheelchair (as I do, especially when not wearing my artificial legs) engenders a feeling of compassion in most others. Sometimes the feeling is a little over-whelming and has to be expressed, in a stooping position, in a loud hectoring voice as though we are hard of hearing and moronic. Sometimes they use the tone adults employ with children. Those confined to wheelchairs have learned to bear with this and the next step, an appraisal in asides. These public airings of sympathy are not regarded as rude, embarrassing or even indiscreet by those whom they are aimed at because the remarks made are so obviously sincere and heartfelt.

Once, when sitting on wheels at a social gathering, I moved a dowager to comment in a huge whisper: "She keeps him clean." This was redeemed by seeing that my glass was kept filled.

Strangely, some people find it hard to address us directly. Often we are referred to in the third person. 1 have been known, obliquely, as Mrs. Cottam's husband. A dentist, having inserted my new top clackers, held up the hand mirror and told me to grin into it so that I could view the results of his handiwork. Reticent to ask for my own cosmetic approval he turned to my wife and asked her opinion.

If I am dragged to a doctor and checked over with a stethoscope, my wife will be asked: "How has he been keeping lately?" The sort of question a vet would ask a keeper.

When the object of a free discussion, or if spoken of in the third person, I release an inane grin and feign a casualness. I do not respond aggressively to these people who are, after all, genuinely concerned about me. I cherish my group 'c' classification (disabled section), even though it is self-bestowed.

Recently I came very close to being re-classified. If I had have lost my temper, I would instantly have been labelled an aggressive type of disabled person.

My wife and I had slipped into a pub for a quick snack. I waddled over to the only vacant gap in a length of wall-bench seating while Dot went to the bar to order sandwiches for two and a beer for one. Sidling stiff-legged between the crowded tables I reached the wall, swivelled, propped my sticks, Wyatt Earped both knee locks and sat down close to a man who was roughly my own age. There was just enough room left for little Dot on my other side.

My near neighbour was impressive with neglected health. His eyes were pale and watery and his cheeks had an unhealthy rosy hue. Thin strands of red veins mapped his nose. Blearily stubbing out a half-inch dog end in the ash tray that we shared geographically he lifted his pint glass, took a swig, placed the glass back on the table and lit another cigarette. Holding it near his mouth in the 'V' of two main fingers he said hoarsely: "You've been in the wars."

"Literally," I said, hoping to nip a conversation before it got going.

Dot broke through the ranks guarding the semi-circular bar against all intruders in the fashionably darkened, crowded room. Carrying my pint, which was in a straight glass, as if it were a vase of flowers, she set it down carefully in front of me and threaded her way back to the bar to wait for the sandwiches.

The liveliness of the froth on the collar of the beer, caused by its self-propellant additive, had barely time to subside as I quickly picked up my drink. The man was threatening to cough over it. He coughed from his roots. He leaned back after this spate of coughing and re-inserted his cigarette. His cheeks hollowed as he sucked on it. Looking askant at my trousered legs he said abruptly through chewed smoke, "I couldn't live with that." That unexpected admission promptly gained him a group 'a' classification (able-bodied section)

He had the sagging posture of one who spent many hours of many days sitting there musing and passing judgements. He drew on his fag, clutched his pint and stared into his beer, the font of his wisdom. His concentration was intense as if he was trying to calculate the depth of the centre of pressure from the surface of the liquid.

"No, I couldn't live with that," he pronounced taking a pull at his pint and washing down exhaling smoke. "I just could not!"

This has in the past been implied by a few like-minded people who also had not contemplated the grim alternative. However, it never had been so bluntly expressed.

"How long have you had them?" he then asked.

"A few years," I said, voluntarily adding that I have had artificial legs for three times longer than I had the original pair. I hoped by this admission to dismiss a topic long ago robbed of novelty. Brain locked in low gear he struggled with his arithmetic, his lips moving silently.

"Bloody 'ell! I'd have done myself in!"

"We all have our burdens to carry," I hinted, an edge to my voice. The man then assumed an insultingly superior look so I decided to wind him up. I know I ought to apologise for this but I cannot do so sincerely. I felt forced to do something to try and stop him from annoying me.

"It has certain advantages, you know, being like this," I said mysteriously.

"Like wot?"

"When, say, I am in a supermarket pushing a trolley for my wife to load, I stare at people and roll my head as I stagger along. They make way allowing us to get to the checking-out till first." I gave him a sample violent stare with a loose roll of the head.

I think he believed me. He drained his glass through his stained teeth and set it down. He stood up and regarded me with more rancour than interest. Bending his head confidingly he whispered: "I'll say this for you."

"Wot?" I asked in easy imitation.

"You're round the bloody twist!" he announced with a bitter smile.

Now utterly dismayed by the blinkered thinking behind his crass remarks, I smiled back widely. Watching him as he shambled towards the door I reflected on a sad quirk of human nature that had just been underlined. We seem to gain comfort at the sight of someone whom we consider to be much worse off than ourselves.

I had just realised, with a stab of guilt, that the departing man had comforted me.

F. T. Cottam,
Tekainga,
31, Fismes Way,
Whitchurch Road,
Wem,
Shropshire,
SY4 SYD.
Tel: 01939-235050

The British Cemetary, Hollain, Belgium.
The author, Eric Cottam visiting the graves of ex-comrades in May 2001.

ACKNOWLEDGEMENTS

I am deeply grateful to the late Squadron Leader Len Pittendrigh for encouraging me to complete this book.

A special thanks to the Public Record Office, Kew, for granting me access to the War Diary (1939-40) of the 2nd. Battalion Royal Warwickshire Regiment.

The History of the Royal Warwickshire Regiment by Marcus Cunliffe also proved to be extremely helpful in confirming where I served in the early days of the Second World War.